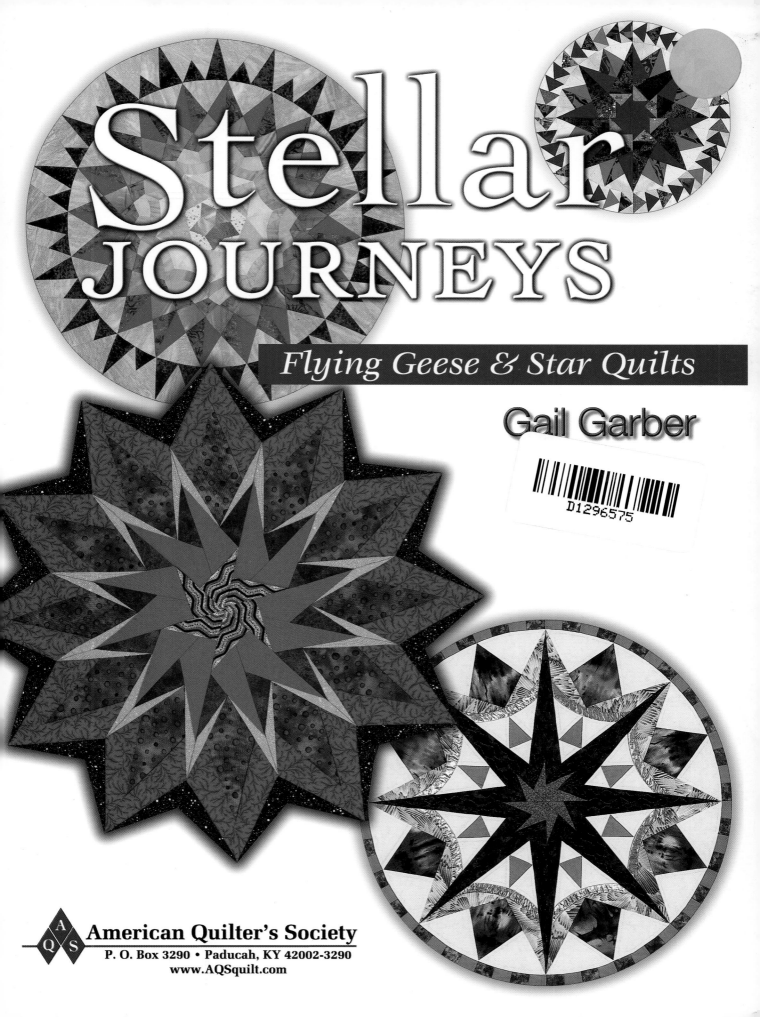

Stellar JOURNEYS

Flying Geese & Star Quilts

Gail Garber

American Quilter's Society

P. O. Box 3290 • Paducah, KY 42002-3290

www.AQSquilt.com

Located in Paducah, Kentucky, the American Quilter's Society (AQS) is dedicated to promoting the accomplishments of today's quilters. Through its publications and events, AQS strives to honor today's quiltmakers and their work and to inspire future creativity and innovation in quiltmaking.

EDITOR: BARBARA SMITH
GRAPHIC DESIGN: LISA M. CLARK
COVER DESIGN: MICHAEL BUCKINGHAM
PHOTOGRAPHY: CHARLES R. LYNCH

Library of Congress Cataloging-in-Publication Data
Garber, Gail
  Stellar Journeys : flying geese & star quilts / by Gail Garber.
        p. cm.
      ISBN 1-57432-775-5
  1. Patchwork--Patterns. 2. Star quilts. 3. Quilting. I. Title.
    TT835 .G3665 2001
746.46'041--dc21   2001004041

Additional copies of this book may be ordered from the American Quilter's Society, PO Box 3290, Paducah, KY 42002-3290, or online at www.AQSquilt.com.

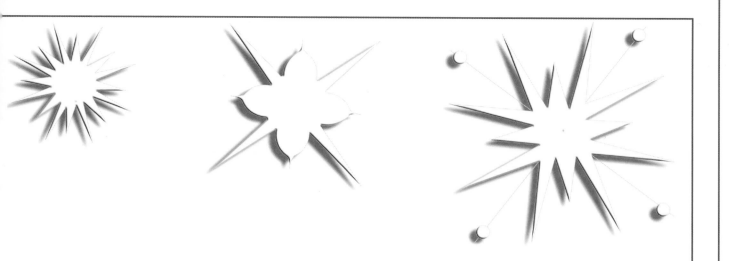

Dedication

This book is dedicated to my daughters, Christi and Tracy. They are beautiful, strong women and an inspiration to me.

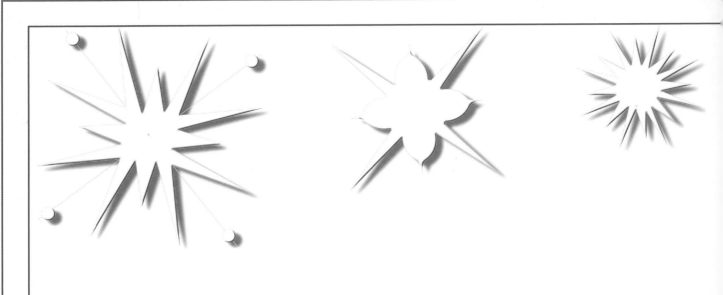

Acknowledgments

Thanks to the wonderful women who made this book possible. The inspiration of many students who have taken the ideas I presented in class and incorporated them into wonderful quilts and quilted clothing over the years has been truly rewarding.

I would like to extend a special thanks to the women who were an inspiration to work with and encouraging throughout the process:

Donna Barnitz, Alice Bessler, Cathy Combs, Pat Drennan, Helen Duncan, Page Gettman, Susie Gray, Michele Hymel, Anita McSorley, Dee Millard, Kathy Morris, Lidy Rekker, and Harriet Smith. Ann Silva generously donated classroom space and sewing machines at her Albuquerque shop, Bernina Sewing Center. Donna Barnitz, Marianne Mershon, and Anita McSorley helped test patterns and text and offered good-natured moral support.

This book is all about group effort and group support.

Contents

In the Beginning

As *novices*, we generally focus on learning a skill before we *dare* to experiment. This is exactly how I *developed* as a *quiltmaker*.

My first quilt was a basic sampler, hand-pieced and hand-quilted in earth tones with plain muslin as the background. It was typical of the rest of the quilts made circa 1980. Sound familiar to your experience?

At class each week, I learned a new skill and new blocks. It took nine months to complete this basic sampler, and we used archaic techniques rarely taught today. We learned to make templates of thick plastic. Our fabric was placed on a sheet of sandpaper to hold it in place while we drew around the templates with a pencil. Scissors were our only cutting tool, and sewing machines were frowned on by "traditional" quilters. It was about five years before I switched to machine piecing.

Early Projects

In 1993, I saw a quilt stitched by Jinny Beyer. It was called RAY OF LIGHT MEDALLION, and I thought it was the most beautiful quilt I had ever seen. More than anything, I wanted a quilt like that for myself. I joined one of my quilt guild's work-study groups, called appropriately "Medallion." The group leader, a staunch traditionalist, led us through basic design techniques

Mine was to be
my *masterpiece* . . .
it would be
beautiful
as well as *huge.*

AZIMUTH
1984 – 1989
110" x 110"
Made by the author.

using compass and pencil. Mine was to be my masterpiece, designed to incorporate a blue and rust paisley stripe and fit my king-sized bed. It would be beautiful as well as huge. And, every stitch would be by hand. Each step of the quilt was designed and hand-stitched before I moved on to the next section.

After the top had been completed, I carefully layered the quilt sandwich and began hand-quilting. My teacher told me that one could never put too much quilting in a quilt. At the time, it seemed like a great idea to stitch around the inside and outside of every paisley in the innermost border. It was only later, when I was quilting the outermost border with exponentially more paisleys, that I questioned this decision.

After five years, in 1989 AZIMUTH was finished, and it is still one of my favorites. Much of that time, the quilt was wadded up in the closet because I was stumped by a design problem or just couldn't bear to work on it any longer. It was during these times that I began drawing small stars that were to become the basis for my designs today.

AZIMUTH featured my interpretation of the traditional Mariner's Compass block. Mariner's Compass is based on a circle that has been divided into pie-shaped wedges. It occurred to me that, if I divided a circle into pie-shaped wedges, I could then draw any number of lines within the wedge. My design would not be a traditional compass but rather an original star.

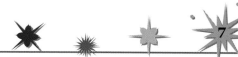

This small quilt was designed by my sister and me . . . she helped me with the drawing as well as insisting that we work accurately.

ANASAZI STAR
1986
23" x 23"
Machine pieced by the author and
hand quilted by Margaret Prina.

Growing as an Artist

About this time, I read about a quilt-block challenge. Each entry had to be a star design. So I gathered my courage and launched into a new quilting era. Fortunately, my first attempt at design garnered a first-place ribbon. I was encouraged to continue my pursuit of original star designs. With each passing project, I learned new skills:

- How to use fabrics and colors that were beyond my comfort zone
- How to create with a limited palette
- How to work within a size constraint
- How to meet deadlines

The small quilt, ANASAZI STAR, was designed by my sister, Ann Rhodes, and me. She is an engineer, and she helped me with the drawing as well as insisting that we work accurately. Our finished drawing featured 10 points spinning around a center. The center is a pentagon, created by combining two points into one. This trick eliminates the bulk of 10 seams that meet in one spot. This star has another slick trick. The points on one side of the wedge do not meet those on the adjoining wedge – fewer points to match.

At that time in my *quilting*,
I generally chose
one focal print *fabric*
with several *colors*
and then selected everything
else to *coordinate*
with that one fabric.

Rocky Mountain Star
1987
24" x 24"
Machine pieced and hand-quilted by the author.

The challenge quilt Rocky Mountain Star came about after meeting Klaudeen Hansen, a nationally known quilter from Wisconsin. I was her hostess when she taught for our guild, and it was my pleasure to spend several days showing her my favorite places in New Mexico. Klaudeen told me about her Wisconsin guild challenge. With great confidence from my first experience, I signed up as a participant. In this challenge, everyone received one piece of fabric that had to be used in the design. When I opened my package, I was less than thrilled with the fabric. At that time in my quilting, I generally chose one focal print fabric with several colors and then selected everything else to coordinate with that one fabric. Now, I was faced with a black fabric with very muted shades of mauve and a teal-blue. I had no idea how to make this work. In the end, I used the challenge fabric in the background and hand-dyed cotton gradations in shades of blue and pink for my star. This time, the star had gentle curves. I also added a simple pieced border.

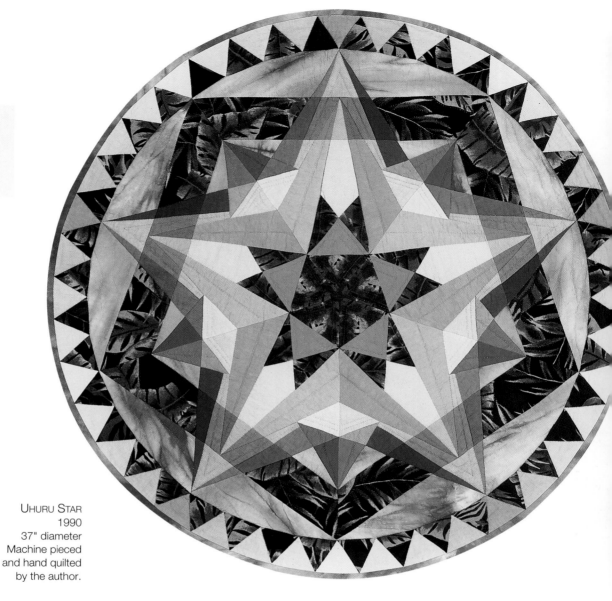

Uhuru means *freedom* in Swahili.

UHURU STAR
1990
37" diameter
Machine pieced
and hand quilted
by the author.

UHURU STAR was also a challenge quilt. It resulted from a meeting with Holice Turnbow, one of the Hoffman Challenge Coordinators. He was visiting Albuquerque, New Mexico, to participate in a quilt symposium in 1989. He told me all about a challenge and even showed me the fabric before I signed up. The fabric, called Jungle Madness, was interesting with its shades of green and bright purple zebras cavorting through the vegetation. It represented a dual challenge for me. Green was definitely not one of the colors in my palette, and the print was much larger than I was accustomed to using. Besides, there were those zebras throughout the print. In the end, I combined shades of teal, purple, and blue hand-dyed cottons along with a prominent band of the challenge fabric woven behind a five-pointed star. At a loss as to how to incorporate the zebras, I carefully cut around them so they did not appear in my design.

NEW WORLD STAR SAMPLER
1990
80" x 80"
Machine pieced and quilted by
the author and Leta Brazell.

Following a meeting with Sandy Muckenthaller, a representative of Hoffman California Fabrics, I received a wonderful sampler of their fabrics to use. I selected one fabric, and Sandy sent a generous assortment of coordinating fabrics. It was like Christmas for me the day the package arrived. I set to work, creating NEW WORLD STAR SAMPLER. I was just learning to machine quilt, and while I tried valiantly to do my best, in the end, the free-form quilting eluded me. Leta Brazell saved the day and the quilt by finishing all the free-motion quilting.

RED OR GREEN?
1999
Machine pieced and appliquéd by the author, Jeanette Gillies, Marion Manson, Nancy McAslan, Anita McSorley, and Donna Ward. Machine quilted by author.

RED OR GREEN? is the result of a round robin between United States and New Zealand. It began in 1997, when I was teaching at their national symposium. At the time, round robin quilts were the rage in the United States, but they were unheard of in New Zealand. My friends and I had just completed a round-robin project, and I had plenty of photos. Several of the New Zealand quilters thought it would be just the thing for the 1999 symposium. The tops were passed back and forth over the Pacific, with each quiltmaker adding to the project.

The theme of each quilt top was to be something about our home state. New Mexico is famous for its fiery foods, and our state vegetable is the chile. Food orders in local restaurants are almost always followed with the question, "Red or green?" The waitress is asking, "Do you want your food smothered with red or green chile sauce?" Our local quilt shops are filled with bolt upon bolt of chile fabrics. A quick trip to the local shop and I was set with four different chile fabrics and coordinates in bright red, orange, yellow, and green. It would be the challenge to end all challenges. Secretly, I thought that it just might be the ugliest quilt ever. I was thrilled when I saw my completed quilt top, hand delivered by Marion Manson, my Kiwi friend.

The Design Group

The original group of Designing Women was formed in 1994. I had just returned from a trip to Alaska where I had agreed to participate in another challenge, this time to write a book for Animas Publishing. It would be about stars and would use the blocks I created for my advanced block of the month class. Eight daring women accepted my challenge to go beyond the class boundaries and explore original star design and original settings for the standard class blocks.

We became fast friends as we helped each other grow as artists. The group functions as both a critique and support group. We've celebrated individual triumphs and helped one another during times of crisis. We have exhibited our work locally and in other states. For many of these quilters, this was their incentive to push their boundaries, enter competitions, and travel. We select themes for different years and work on different types of projects, from simple to complex. The group has now grown to 14, although not all of the original members still belong. Each member has designed and stitched a quilt or quilted garment for this book. For some, it represents a first quilt. It has been a real pleasure to work with each one, and I am certain that this book would not exist without their help, advice, and encouragement.

Eight daring *women*
accepted my challenge
to go *beyond* the class *boundaries*
and explore original
star design
and original settings
for the *standard* class blocks.

The group proudly displays SYNESTHESIA, the quilt they stitched in secret, from Gail. They entered it anonymously in the local quilt show judged by Gail to see what she really thought about the quilt. It won "Best Use of Color." Pictured from left to right: Cathy Combs, Kathy Morris, Dee Millard, Susie Gray, Lorraine Quinn, Harriet Smith, Helen Duncan, Gail Garber, Anita McSorley, Page Gettman, Pat Drennan, Michele Hymel. Not shown: Mary Chappelle and Lisa Stewart.

Chapter 1

Let's
Get
Started

Tools of the Trade

The correct equipment, in good working order, makes all the difference in the world when it comes to success in making a project. I hear from my students and have personally experienced the joy of seeing my sewing skills increase immeasurably upon getting a new, high-quality sewing machine. Suddenly, all the stitches that were impossible on my old machine were sewn with perfection on my new one. Sewing became much more pleasurable, and the end products were more professional. It happened almost overnight! The old sewing machine now lives at my daughter's home, where it continues to function adequately as long as one doesn't try to zigzag or make buttonholes.

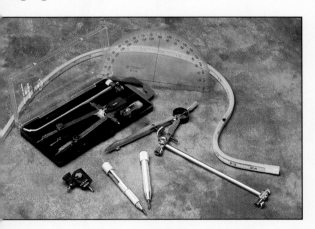

Treat yourself to good tools. The following items are essential for drawing blocks:

Compass

Every quilter who designs his or her own quilts should have a good compass with an extender bar for drawing large circles. These compasses lock in place so you don't have to worry about them slipping. Compasses can be found in art- or office-supply stores, or if you are lucky, you'll find a free one. Most engineers and draftsmen have an old set they used in college that has never been out of its box since then. I've acquired two sets this way. The small compasses designed for school use slip during drawing. They are not accurate and do not extend far enough to make large circles.

Compass Points

Compass points are sold in art-supply stores and some quilt shops. These points attach to a yardstick and can be used to draw circles up to 70" in diameter. There are two disadvantages. It has a dull pivot point and a very wide lead. However, it is the only tool for drawing really large circles. Find a friend to hold the center while you draw the circle.

Inking Attachment

This small jewel of a tool enables you to attach a mechanical pencil or a pen to the compass. No more struggles with those fat pieces of lead, which are never sharp enough. Look for this gadget in an art-supply store.

Rotary Cutting Mat

Place your rotary cutting mat under the paper before you begin to draw a design. It provides a stable, self-healing surface for the compass point. No more nicks in the table.

Protractor

A protractor is used for accurately measuring angles. My favorite is made from one piece of plastic with no hole cut from the center. Because there is one solid piece of plastic, the protractor is more stable.

Flexible Curve

I use this tool to create sweeping curves that need to be similar, such as the roughly parallel lines forming a row of flying geese. It is also helpful for making landscape and skyscape curves. Try to find one that is at least 18" to 24" long. Shorter flexible curves must be moved frequently for drawing, so it is more challenging to achieve a smooth transition between sections.

Mechanical Pencil

Use a mechanical pencil for drawing all patterns. The width of the lead is fixed. I've seen several projects run into trouble because of the wide lines of an old-fashioned wooden pencil. If you must use a wooden pencil, keep the point sharp.

Good Eraser

We all make mistakes. Make it easier to change your drawing by using a large easily held eraser. Art gum erasers erase completely and quickly.

Drawing Paper

Graph paper is not necessary because the lines you will be drawing usually will not correspond with those on graph paper. The minimum drawing paper size that I recommend is 17" x 22". I prefer to use 22" x 34". Standard newsprint (unprinted, of course) works well and can be purchased in pads at an art- or office-supply store. I buy roll ends of plain newsprint from the local newspaper publisher. Each roll is five feet wide and 50 to 100 yards long. These multi-purpose rolls are also great for kids' drawings, school banners, and packing material for shipping boxes. No home should be without one.

Rulers

Compare your rulers with each other. They should all measure the same. Sometimes, one side has a perfect quarter inch while the other is slightly larger or smaller. If this is the case, mark the "good" side so that it is easily identifiable. Also check the ends of the ruler for accuracy.

All rulers are not created equal. Make sure that those you use in a project measure the same. If possible, use the same ruler throughout a project. An 18" see-through ruler is necessary, not only for drawing the basic lines, but also for adding the ¼" seam allowances to your templates.

A 12" or 16" square ruler is valuable because it creates perfect squares, which are a must for success. In addition, I like to lay my star pieces out, right side up in the correct order, on the 16" square ruler. Then I can easily see their correct arrangement while I'm sewing. This ruler is also convenient for carrying pieces back and forth from the ironing board to the sewing machine.

A 4" square ruler is my favorite for drawing short lines. It fits nicely in the hand and is easy to maneuver. I also use it to cut around small templates. When I am paper foundation piecing, it is the perfect size for trimming the finished piece and adding the ¼" seam allowance, all at one time.

Freezer Paper

I love freezer paper for paper foundation piecing. After I have sewn two fabric pieces in place, I flip the new piece back and press with a dry iron. The waxy side of the freezer paper adheres to the wrong side of the fabric and prevents it from pleating or puckering when the next piece is added. Freezer paper is just as easy to remove as tissue paper and much more durable. It will hold up through ripping and re-stitching.

Neutral-Colored Thread

For sewing over different colors of fabric, I find that a medium gray thread blends with most colors. I also recommend only high-quality cotton sewing threads for your piecing projects. The thread sold at several spools per dollar is less durable and often breaks during sewing. It also leaves a lint in the sewing machine.

Double-Napped Flannel

A two-yard piece of white flannel tacked to a wall makes a quick, easy, and removable flannel board. Cotton adheres to flannel. I like to stick my cut pieces to the flannel and then step back to view them before sewing. This gives me a fairly good idea of how the finished star will look.

Spray Adhesive

You will want a "re-stickable" spray glue, similar to that found on post-it notes. I use it to spray the back of my paper templates before attaching them to thin cardboard. This method makes a durable template, which can later be thrown away. A nice feature of this glue is that, if you make an error, the paper can simply be lifted and re-applied. I do not recommend permanent spray glues.

Using Color

Strong contrast makes successful quilts. I am pleased with my quilts if the basic design is evident from across a large room. This tells me that I have enough contrast between the sections to allow each element to stand out in the quilt. Contrast may be the most important element in an effective quilt design. After all, when you spend hours and hours working on a quilt, you want people to be able to see the design.

Binoculars are the perfect tool to determine if there is enough contrast in your quilt. Pin your quilt parts to a wall or flannel board or lay them out on the floor. Step as far away from them as possible and raise the wrong end of the binoculars to one eye while closing the other eye. Your quilt will appear to be far away, and the image will be darker. You should still be able to see the design elements clearly.

The Scrappy Star Quilt

In this type of quilt, the stars are individually color coordinated but may not bear any resemblance to each other. My theory is that, in space, objects are independent of one another and therefore would not be alike in color or design. An object in space is often in conflict with, or on a collision course with, another object. This idea is represented by the use of warm and cool colors for different stars.

The backgrounds in this type of quilt are almost entirely scrappy. The use of many fabrics creates the illusion of motion. While the overall effect reads as background, there are enough different fabrics to capture the eye and prevent it from completely passing over the background. Divide your background fabrics into color values of dark, medium, and light. Assuming that the star generates light, place the lightest background fabrics nearest the star, gradually fading to dark. My backgrounds tend to be shades of blue, gray, and black.

Space is not empty. I fill in the background with scrappy geese because this adds to the effect that something is going on even in the darkest areas. Only occasionally, do I use a solid piece of fabric, and then only in a small area.

Flying geese can be used to create motion in a star quilt. If you want it to appear that the star is in motion, trailed by geese, use some of the colors from the star in the geese and the scrappy background behind the geese. Place the lightest geese closest to the star. See REDONDO on page ??.

The Color-Coordinated Star

For many of my quilts, especially those in which I want a homogenous effect, I use a formula that works well for me. I begin by choosing one fabric and then selecting others that complement it. This type of quilt is generally color-coordinated throughout, with a blend of colors, color values, and textures. For a sampler-type quilt, I generally use one or two focal fabrics, eight to 10 accent fabrics, one to 10 background fabrics, and sometimes a zinger.

Hand-dyed, Hand-painted Fabrics

These versatile fabrics can be used to create a variety of illusions. I really like hand-painted fabrics that fade from one color to another. I use these in long rows of geese like those in COSMIC PARADE on page 65. The geese gradually change color as the fabric changes. Also, if there is a vein of one color in the hand-painted fabric, it will show through in the geese, enhancing the curve effect. Hand-dyed gradations are effective when used to create motion through the placement of shades of one color, such as the borders in SPRING and AUTUMN on pages 63 and 64.

Focal Fabric

These often have several colors within the same print and can be either large or medium in scale. They may be floral or geometric, or they may contain simple swirls of colors. These fabrics are often the basis for a quilt, because you can choose other fabrics based on the colors in the focal print. I often begin a geometric star with one of these prints. Because a focal fabric is often a large print, the design may repeat less often than a small print, possibly only once every 18". It is also likely that this fabric may be used throughout a larger quilt, acting as the connector between sections and possibly as part or all of the border.

Selective cutting or isolating a print creates wonderful circular designs in an area where several identical pieces meet, as in the center of a star. To achieve this effect, find one part of a medium or large print or a stripe that you think will look good in an area like this. Find enough repeats of this exact area of the print. Cut each piece from the exact same area of the print.

Selective cutting requires a disproportionally large amount of fabric. You will end up with a large piece that looks like swiss cheese, with odd shapes missing throughout.

Color Value

A successful quilt will have a blend of light, medium, and dark colors. These can be either prints or solids. Avoid selecting colors that coordinate too closely because, from a distance, these will appear to be the same fabric.

Texture

Again, avoid careful coordination of fabrics. Choose a variety of textures for your quilt. This means small, medium, and large prints. Different textures add interest. Quilts that include the same size and texture of prints may appear to be plain, even with a good blend of colors.

Solids

Wonderfully colorful quilts can be made entirely with solid-colored fabrics. Close attention to color placement, contrast, and value are essential. Solids can also be used as accent fabrics or for textural contrast with other prints in the quilt.

Accent Fabrics

These are fabrics that more or less coordinate with a focal fabric. Choose several of these. You will probably find the fabric you have the least of will quickly become your favorite, and you'll wish you had purchased more.

Zinger

This is one fabric that doesn't match the others in your quilt. It may be from the opposite side of the color wheel, such as a burst of orange in an otherwise lavender and purple quilt. Zingers add interest to your quilt. They catch one's eye and say, "I'm here! Look at me!"

Quality Fabrics

The quilt you are now stitching may be the one to last 100 years. That is, it may be if you use high-quality, 100-percent cotton fabrics. Often, the process of making a quilt can take anywhere from 40 to 1,000 hours of careful planning and stitching. Your work will be enhanced and your project more enjoyable if you treat yourself to fine quality fabric. Support your local quilt shop. This is the shop that caters to your needs and has a wide range of cottons in every hue imaginable. The quilt shop's prices per yard may be higher because the quality is greater (higher thread count). Also, the shop owner buys in smaller quantities than discount or chain stores, therefore, a small store can carry a wide range of different fabrics. A quilt shop is also the place where you can receive free, custom services, like assistance with figuring yardage, fabric selection, and the latest tips and techniques to make your project successful.

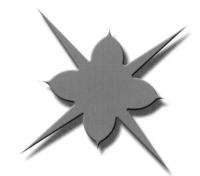

Chapter 2

Making Star and Geese Quilts

Drawing Circular Stars

It's much easier than you might think to draw your own circular stars. Before you begin, mentally let go of any predetermined notions about what the finished block will look like. This will enable you to concentrate on each step, one at a time, without worrying about what will happen further along.

It's always a good idea to make several practice drawings to develop an understanding for the process before you begin drawing a full-sized pattern. I like to draw practice blocks that measure 6" in diameter. Any that turn out well can easily be enlarged to a 12" or 18" block. Also, the 6" block can be drawn on an 8½" x 11" sheet of paper with a small compass.

It is not necessary to use graph paper for drawing stars because most drawn lines will not correspond to the grid on the paper. Often the grid is not perfectly square. If you rely on paper like this, it can distort your star, making it impossible to create accurate templates.

Before you begin, refer to Figure 2–1, which shows several different angles as well as a circle's diameter and radius. These terms are used frequently in the instructions.

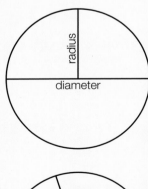

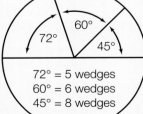

72° = 5 wedges
60° = 6 wedges
45° = 8 wedges

Figure 2–1.

Tips

1. Avoid drawing a lot of lines that come together in a point. These make very narrow points that are nearly impossible to sew.

2. It's easy to draw something on paper that is impossible to sew. Avoid intersections with pesky pivot points (set-in seams).

3. Avoid drawing tiny pieces that disappear into the design and which are nearly impossible to sew. If you can't hold them easily in your fingers, they are unnecessary.

Basic Drawing

Begin by making a base line to represent the diameter of your circle. Make a tiny dot to identify the exact center. For example, if your finished circle measures 6", there should be 3" on each side of the center mark (Figure 2–2).

3"   •   3"

Figure 2–2.

Use a compass to draw the circle, as follows: Place the point of the compass on the center dot. Open the compass so the pencil point reaches one end of the base line, in this example, 3". I find it is more accurate to draw the line first, rather than the circle. Then I use the line to determine how wide to open the compass. Draw a circle around the center dot (Figure 2–3).

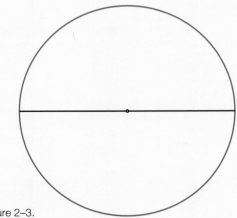

Figure 2–3.

Decide how many wedges to use in your star. You can use any number, but your design will be easier to draw and piece if you choose a number that divides evenly into 360°. Divide 360° by the number of wedges you want in your star. For example, if your star has eight wedges, then the angle of each wedge will be 45°, six wedges will be 60°, five wedges will be 72°.

Use your protractor to mark the angles except 45° (see Drawing 45˚ Wedges). Align the protractor with the base line and match the center dot on the line with the 90° mark on the protractor. Mark each section on the circle, creating the necessary number of wedge sections. To finish drawing each wedge, align your ruler so it passes through the center dot and the marks on both sides of the circle. Connect these points (Figure 2–4).

Figure 2–5 shows a circle divided into five equal sections. Note that, when a circle is divided into five wedges, one half of the base line needs to be erased.

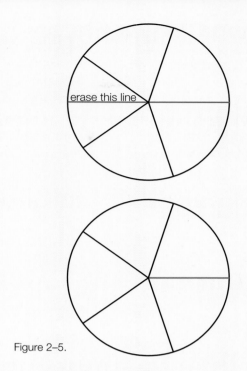

Figure 2–5.

Drawing 45° Wedges

Draw a base line and a circle. Use your protractor to mark the 90° angles and draw lines dividing the circle into four equal sections, labeled A, B, C, and D in Figure 2–6.

Use your compass to divide the circle into eight equal sections, as follows: Open the compass so it measures more than half way between A and B.

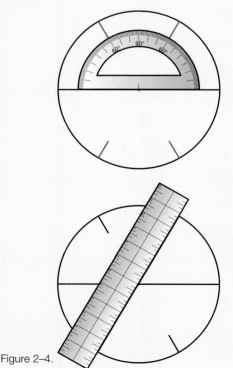

Figure 2–4.

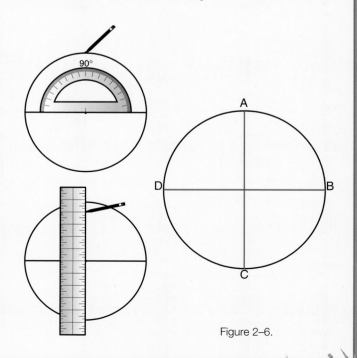

Figure 2–6.

Place the point at intersection A. Mark small arcs on the outside of the circle on both sides of intersection A. Then mark small arcs on both sides of intersection B (Figure 2–7). Continue marking small arcs at intersections C and D. The arcs will cross, forming an X at the exact center of each wedge section. Be careful to keep your compass from slipping or widening. If this happens, the sections will not be divided equally.

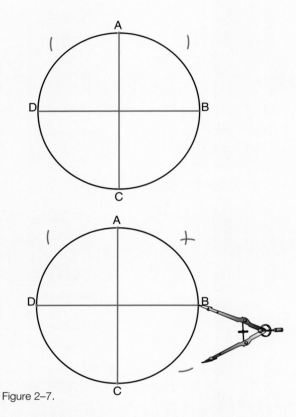

Figure 2–7.

If the compass is not opened wide enough, then there will be no intersecting arcs (Figure 2–9).

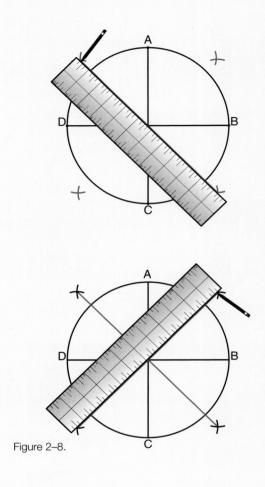

Figure 2–8.

Use your ruler and a pencil to connect the X's on opposite sides of the circle through the circle's center dot (Figure 2–8). This method can be used to divide sections into even smaller wedges. It is significantly more accurate than measuring with a protractor, especially for very narrow angles.

If your compass is opened too wide when making the arcs, the X formed will be far outside the circle. For a very large star, the X's on opposite sides of the circle may be so far apart that a ruler cannot span the distance between them.

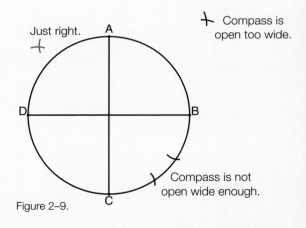

Figure 2–9.

Many designs require that each wedge be divided one or more times. Use the compass/arc marking method to continue dividing the wedges (Figure 2–10 on the following page).

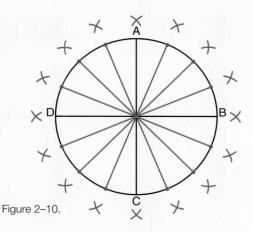

Figure 2–10.

ps:
If the ruler does not pass through the X's on oppo-
e sides of the circle and the center of the drawing,
en at least one of the angles is incorrect. Measure
ch angle again to make sure it is the correct num-
r of degrees. It is essential to draw accurately.

Keep your drawing clean. Erase base lines and
cs after they are no longer needed. As you add
w dividing lines and measurements, a drawing can
come cluttered and confusing if you don't erase
tra lines as you go.

Playing Within the Wedge

Before you begin to draw within a wedge, you
will need to decide if you prefer to use paper
foundations (page 28) or template piecing
(page 29) and modify your drawing accordingly.
There are limitations with paper foundation
piecing. Curved seams cannot be foundation
pieced. Set-in seams and some other types of
intersections do not lend themselves to foundation piecing. Carefully review your drawing to
be certain that it can be foundation pieced. You
may need to revise your drawing to eliminate
difficult piecing.

Now the fun part begins. You will need a ruler,
compass, and protractor. Working with one of
the wedges, add some lines inside it. For example, let's say you want to draw a line from the
halfway point of the wedge to the outside edge.
First, determine the measurement of a point
that is one-fourth of the diameter. If your circle

measures 6", then this measurement would be
1½". Open your compass to that measurement
and lightly draw a circle inside the larger circle.
This smaller circle will cross a point at the
same distance on each wedge. Next divide the
wedge in half by using your compass to make
arcs as described on page 21 (Drawing 45°
Wedges). Draw a line from the edge of the inner
circle on each side of the wedge to the mid-
point on the outer edge (Figure 2–11).

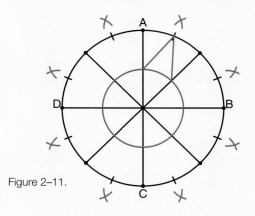

Figure 2–11.

Look at the lines you have just drawn. Do they
look promising? If you like what you have
done, then draw the same lines in the remaining wedges. After you have completed all the
lines, erase the smaller circle, the arcs, and any
other unnecessary marks (Figure 2–12).

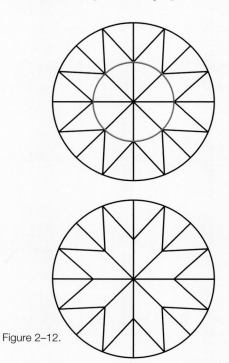

Figure 2–12.

Draw a line across the widest part of each star point, where the inner circle was. The two triangles will be easier to piece than setting in a circular center. Always simplify your drawing if possible (Figure 2–13).

Continue adding lines, one at a time, until you decide your star design is complete (Figures 2–15 and 2–16).

Figure 2–15.

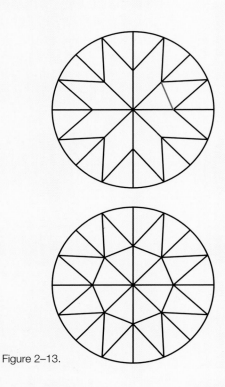

Figure 2–13.

Look at your design and decide where you would like to draw another line. For example, use your compass to mark the same point on each wedge, then draw a line from that point to another point, which can be anywhere inside the wedge. Check to see if you like the new shape you have created. Repeat the same line in each of the remaining wedges (Figure 2–14).

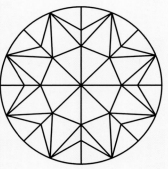

Figure 2–14.

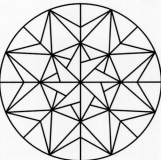

Figure 2–16.

Curves Anyone?

It's easy to insert a curved seam into the wedge of a star. I generally use curves sparingly because of the piecing difficulties they present. However, sometimes one curved seam within a star will greatly improve it. Let's experiment by using a star drawing.

p: Be careful to draw gentle curves that ll not be too difficult to piece. Large ces are easier to handle than small ones. oid small, deep curves.

To draw a curve to replace a straight line, first erase the straight line. Place the point of your compass at the tip of the star where it intersects the circle. Open the compass so the pencil end meets the widest part of the star point. Make an arc across where the straight line had been (Figure 2–17).

Figure 2–18.

Try replacing the outermost wedge lines with a curve. It may be a little more difficult to find a base point, which needs to be somewhere outside the circle. To locate this point, draw an additional circle outside the circular star. Extend the original wedge lines to the new circle. With the compass point at the intersection of the wedge line and the outer circle, make two marks on the outer circle. Use these new marks as base points for the compass and make two new arcs inside the wedge (Figure 2–19).

Figure 2–17.

Do you like this effect? Try making an additional curve that mirrors the first one. Use the same base point for the compass and open the compass a little less wide than before. This double arc forms an accent that highlights the curved effect (Figure 2–18).

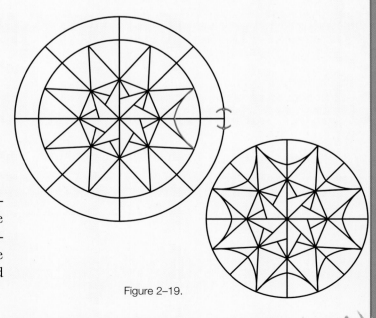

Figure 2–19.

Sewing Your Star

Paper Foundation Piecing

At one time, I steadfastly avoided paper foundation piecing. It seemed slow, cumbersome, and wasteful of fabric, and the final unpleasantry was removing all of the paper. I vowed never willingly to use this technique. My classes were taught with templates and ¼" seam allowances.

However, once I began creating these free-form shapes, in which every piece was a different size, the thought of making individual templates was overwhelming. I was forced to use paper foundations but resented it every stitch of the way. Then a funny thing happened. My students began insisting that paper was better, and they showed me faster ways and tips that made it much easier. They became my teachers.

I learned that paper-foundation piecing is infinitely more accurate than most template piecing, especially for novice sewers. There are drawbacks, however. The paper still has to be removed, and curved seams cannot be paper-foundation pieced. It is slow, but the advantages make this technique my new, favorite way to piece.

Tips:

1. I prefer to use freezer paper for my foundations because fabrics adhere to the waxy side of the paper when pressed. The fabric can also be peeled back for trimming and then re-pressed. This method prevents puckers or bubbles in the finished piece.

2. Do not attempt to put freezer paper through a photocopier or a laser printer. The heat used to set the ink will permanently fuse the layers together.

It is important to remember that paper-foundation piecing creates a mirror image of the drawn design. This means that, if your star spins clockwise on the foundation, it will spin counterclockwise in the finished quilt.

Make your paper foundation from the most accurate section of your star. Number or letter the pieces within the section in the order in which they will be sewn.

Making Foundations

From the original drawing, trace a wedge on the paper (dull) side of a piece of freezer paper. Trace each line within the wedge and transfer the lettering or numbering system to the freezer paper. Cut three additional pieces of freezer paper the same size as the first. Stack them up with the waxy side facing down and place a plain piece of paper under them. Place the traced wedge on the top. With an old, unthreaded needle in your sewing machine, sew each line in the wedge, as well as ¼" outside the edge. Peel the paper foundations apart and transfer the numbering or lettering system to each one. Continue making foundations until you have one for each wedge.

Cutting the Fabric

There are at least two different ways to cut fabric for paper piecing. Accuracy is not essential, and the simplest method is to merely cut a hunk of fabric that is at least an inch larger than the finished size of each piece. This hunk can be stitched and then trimmed.

Pre-cutting fabrics that are approximately the right size makes for more organized piecing and less waste. It requires a little measuring and advanced planning, but it can make the sewing quicker. First, look at the foundation and decide the direction in which successive pieces will flip open after they are sewn. Mark an arrow that points toward the direction of the flip. The direction the arrow points is the height of the patch, and the side touching the bottom of the arrow is the base (Figure 2–20 on the following page).

Measure the height of the patch and the length of the base. Shown are two pieces, A and E, from the wedge pattern on page 53. Because A is surrounded by other patches, it is best to let the fabric grain line run through the center. The grain line of E is best placed on the long edge. The finished size of A is approximately 2⅜" x 6⅛". The finished size of E is approximately ½" x 4⅝" (Figure 2–21). Add a seam allowance to each piece, then add an extra ½" to 1" to both dimensions to allow for the placement and the flip. Round the measurements off to a size that is easily measured and cut the fabric pieces with rotary-cutting equipment.

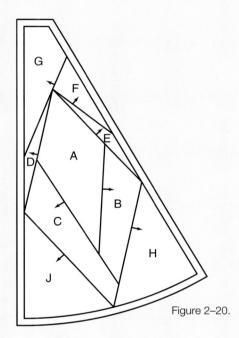

Figure 2–20.

Sometimes the base of a piece is shorter than the other sides. In this instance, it is necessary to cut the fabric piece large enough to cover the longest edge. It may also be necessary to offset the piece when sewing it to the base line, shifting it one direction or the other. I always pin these pieces in place first and have a practice flip to see if the piece will cover the area.

Determining Cutting Size

Piece	Finished Size	With Seam Allowance	Cutting Size
A	2⅜" x 6⅛"	2⅞" x 6⅝"	3½" x 7½"
E	½" x 4½"	1" x 5"	1½" x 5½"

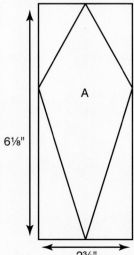

Figure 2–21.

Sewing Paper Foundations

In this type of paper-foundation piecing, you will sew on the paper, and the fabric will be next to the feed dogs on your sewing machine. Sew on the drawn lines.

Position the fabric for piece A, right side up on the wrong side of the freezer paper, making sure that it covers all the seams. Press A in place, touching the hot iron to the right side of the fabric. Then, turn the foundation over and press again, making sure that the iron is touching the paper side of the freezer paper and not the shiny waxy side.

Position piece B over A, right sides together, leaving at least ¼" for the seam allowances. Hold the piece in place, turn the foundation over, and sew on the line between pieces A and B (Figure 2–22). Trim the seam allowances to ¼" (Figure 2–23). Flip B open and press in position (Figure 2–24). Continue the process, adding each successive piece. Trim, flip, and press after sewing each seam (Figures 2–25 to 2–31).

Trim excess fabric that extends beyond the wedge after all the pieces have been attached (Figure 2–32). Remember to leave the ¼" seam allowance around the outside of the wedge. Remove the paper before sewing sections together.

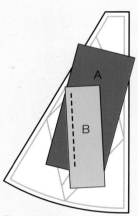

Figure 2–22.

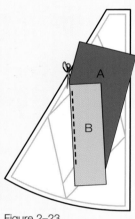

Figure 2–23.

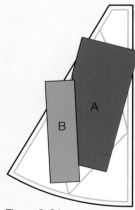

Figure 2–24.

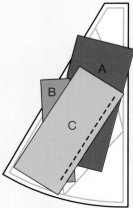

Figure 2–25.

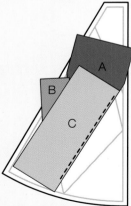

Figure 2–26.

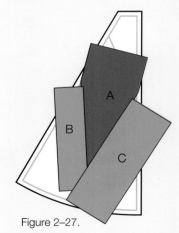

Figure 2–27.

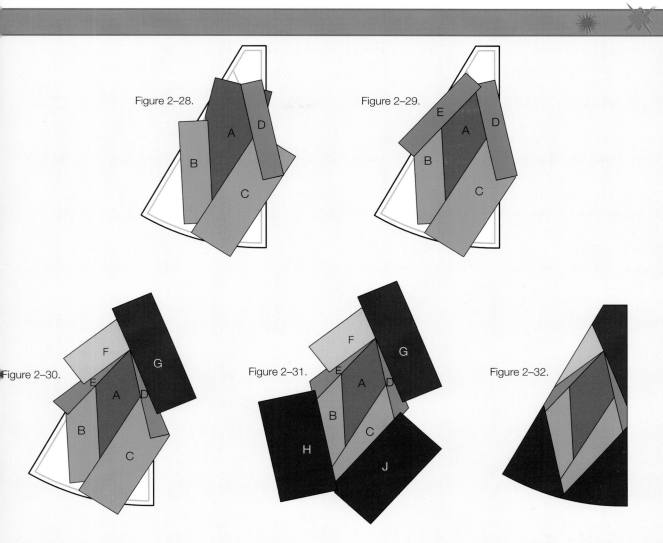

Figure 2–28.

Figure 2–29.

Figure 2–30.

Figure 2–31.

Figure 2–32.

Template Piecing

If you would rather use templates instead of foundations, it is essential that your seam allowance width be precise.

The perfect ¼". When is a ¼" not a ¼"? Throughout my years of teaching, I have seen the ¼" vary from ⅛" to nearly ½", sometimes all within the same block. If you are not certain of your seam allowance, sew ¼" from the edge of a scrap of fabric and then measure the seam allowance width. If it's not exact, adjust your sewing line.

Fixing a less-than-perfect ¼". Circular star designs have several seams that join in the center of each block. This means that any inaccuracies in the seam allowances will be magnified in the center of the block, often creating a "bonnet" or "ruffled edge" rather than a flat block. Seam allowances that are wider than ¼" cause the bonnet effect, while those narrower than ¼" create ruffled edges. Generally, the problem only becomes evident after you have sewn the final seam and the completed star does not lie flat.

Sometimes, if the problem is relatively minor, it can be fixed with careful pressing. First, set the circular star into the background square. At this point, the star can literally be blocked, just like blocking a sweater or blanket. Place a towel flat on an ironing board or other surface that can be wetted. Pin the square so it measures the exact size it should measure. Spray it with plain water until it is thoroughly wet. Cover the block with a clean lightweight piece of fabric and let the block dry. When dry, the block usually conforms to size. I always find this rather amazing, but it does work.

The bonnet effect is more common than ruffled edges. If this is your recurring problem, you might try slightly increasing the amount of seam allowance toward the center of the star as you stitch your wedges together. Begin sewing at the outside of the wedge with a ¼" seam allowance. As you work your way toward the center, gradually increase the seam allowance to about ⅜". Be careful to be consistent when stitching each wedge. The final seam allowance may be somewhat wider than ¼".

Tip: Take the time necessary to perfect your ¼" seam allowance. It will make future quilt piecing projects accurate and much easier to sew.

Making templates. Templates are essential if your star contains any curved seams. Use the most accurate wedge in your drawing to make your templates and make all the templates from the same wedge. Trace each shape on a piece of paper. Label each piece and mark the grain line (Figure 2–33).

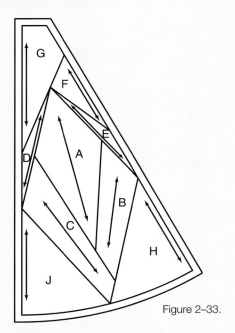

Figure 2–33.

Transfer the grain lines to the templates and add a ¼" seam allowance to each one. Add match marks to all templates that have odd angles so you can match the pieces more easily (Figure 2–34).

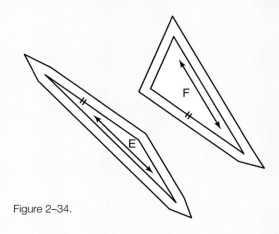

Figure 2–34.

Tip: Adding seam allowances to curved piec is easy with a compass. Place the point of t compass in the original base point. Open t compass so it is ¼" longer than the curv edge of the template and draw the curve.

My favorite way to make templates is simple and accurate. Begin with re-stickable spray glue and a manila file folder or some other thin cardboard, like the side of a cereal box or an insert from a shirt or stockings. Spray the backs of the paper templates and stick them to the cardboard. If you make a mistake, or wrinkle the paper, simply lift it from the cardboard and re-apply. The templates are ready to be cut with a pair of scissors.

Sewing with templates. Place the templates right side up on the right side of the fabrics, except for mirror-image pieces, which will be cut with the fabric folded, wrong sides together. Trace around each template and cut the fabric pieces. Because these shapes can be confusing and can include odd angles, I arrange my pieces in order as I cut them. A 16" square ruler is perfect for this task. It will hold nearly all the pieces necessary for a full star. Stack all like pieces in place on the ruler. This way you can see your color arrangement and make changes if necessary.

Sew fabric pieces together, matching end points and match marks. After a wedge section has been completed, measure to make sure that it is the correct size.

Some wedges may be made from two or more
partial wedges that must be pieced. As shown
in the example in Figure 2–35a and b, sew the
two partial wedges together, and then add the
connecting piece to form the innermost point
of the wedges.

Joining Wedges

Whether the finished wedges have been made
with foundations or with templates, sew them
together in pairs. Join pairs to make quarter circles, then half circles. Press all seam allowances
in the same direction, either clockwise or counterclockwise, to reduce bulk. Sew the two half
circles together to complete a circle (Figure
2–36a and b).

Figure 2–36a.

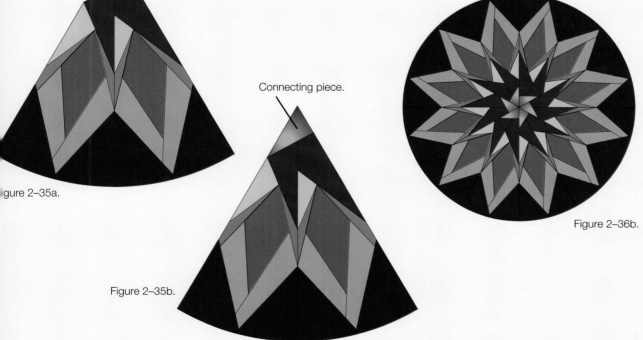

Figure 2–35a.

Connecting piece.

Figure 2–35b.

Figure 2–36b.

Drawing Circular Borders

We've all seen those marvelous quilts, with rows and rows of circular borders forming the perfect frame for a circular star design. They look intimidating, as if they would be nearly impossible to design and sew, but it's much easier than you may think. There are some tricks that help to make planning and sewing circular borders a breeze.

Basic Drawing

Let's assume that your circular block has a 12" diameter with a simple eight-pointed star. Begin by drawing two additional circles outside the original circle. Open your compass to 7½" for the first circle and 9" for the second circle. You now have a 3"-wide border that has been divided in half. Extend the lines dividing the star from the center through the star points to the outer edge of the border. These lines will divide your circular border into eight sections (Figure 2–37). Divide each of the eight border sections in half. To find the center of each section, place your compass point on the outer circle at an intersection with a center line. Open your compass to a point that is wider than halfway between the sections. Make a small arc outside the circle, then swing the compass around to make an arc in the adjacent section (Figure 2–38). Repeat this process at each intersection.

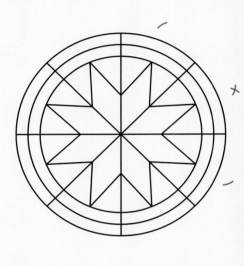

Figure 2–38.

Figure 2–37.

Align your ruler through the X formed by one pair of arcs, through the center of the block, to the X on the opposite side of the drawing. Draw a line through the border sections only. The border will be divided into 16 equal sections (Figure 2–39). Erase the arcs. They might confuse you later on.

You can repeat this process to create even more divisions. Erase the arcs. You now have all the base lines to draw several different border designs. Now it's time to play!

Let's make Flying Geese. Draw one triangular goose. Are you pleased with its shape? If you are happy, then fill in the rest of the border with geese. Erase the circle dividing the border, and your design is finished (Figure 2–41).

Figure 2–41.

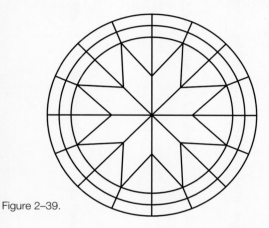

Figure 2–39.

Divide the outer border into 32 sections by using the same method of making arcs between each section (Figure 2–40).

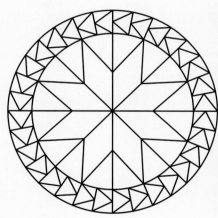

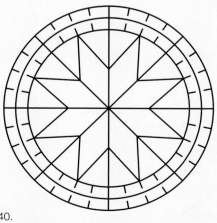

Figure 2–40.

Tip: This border can be paper pieced in sections of four or more geese.

Now, let's try radiating points. This design is really easy. Just draw lines between the inner and outer circles, zigging and zagging between sections (Figure 2–42). Erase all of the section lines and the dividing circle.

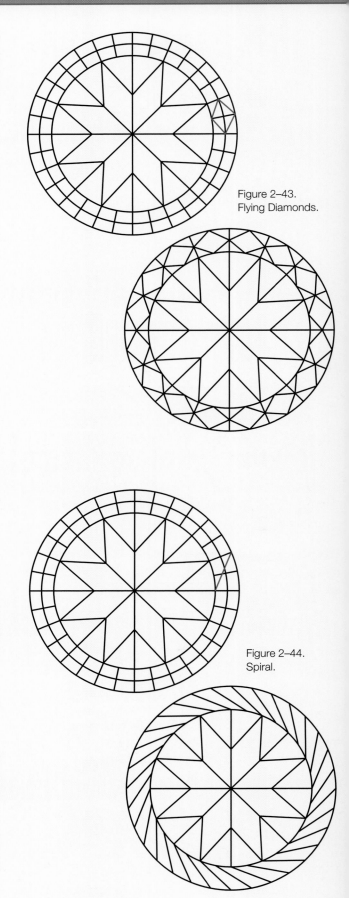

Figure 2–43.
Flying Diamonds.

Figure 2–42.

One of my favorite borders is Flying Diamonds, as shown in Figure 2–43. This design does not lend itself well to paper-foundation piecing, however.

The spiral is among the easiest of borders to draft and to sew (Figure 2–44).

Figure 2–44.
Spiral.

More complex borders can be created by additional divisions of the outer border. Use your compass to divide the circle into 64 sections (Figure 2–45).

The radiating points in Figure 2–46 are narrower and longer and give a completely different look than those shown in Figure 2–42.

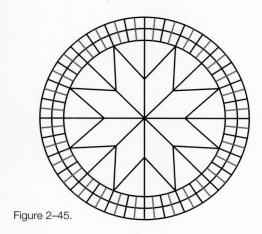

Figure 2–45.

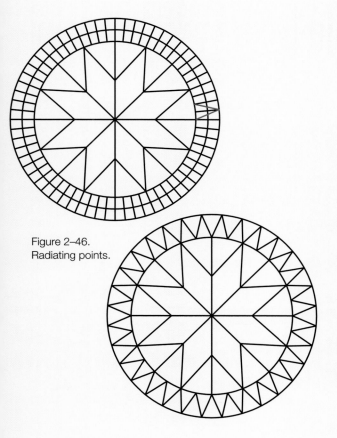

Figure 2–46.
Radiating points.

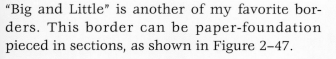

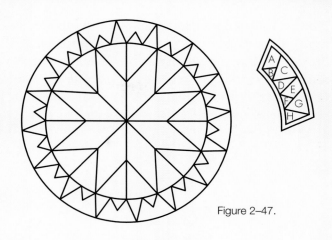

Figure 2–47.

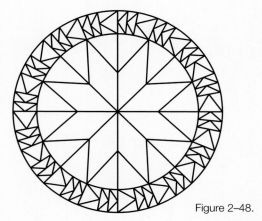

Figure 2–48.

Additional Circular Borders

I often add a plain fabric circle border between pieced borders, which sets the borders apart, accenting each one. It also eliminates many points that must match between the borders. Make a template for one-eighth of a circle. Cut this piece with the grain line "parallel" to the longest edge (Figure 2–49).

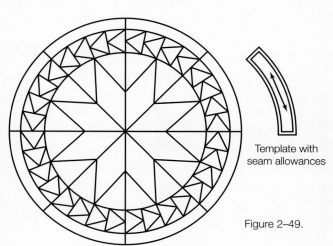

Template with seam allowances

Figure 2–49.

"Big and Little" is another of my favorite borders. This border can be paper-foundation pieced in sections, as shown in Figure 2–47.

Flying Geese take on a new perspective when there are 64 divisions of the circle. Try combining large and small geese in one border (Figure 2–48).

The next outer border will need to be wider to keep the same proportions as the inner border. In the design shown in Figure 2–50, the inner star is 12", and the first circle border is 3" wide. The plain border measures 1" wide, and the outer border measures 4". The finished design is 28" in diameter.

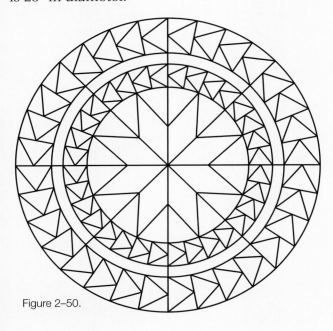

Figure 2–50.

Sewing Borders

Use either paper foundation or template piecing techniques to make your border. Divide the border into small sections that can be easily assembled. For instance, if the center star has eight wedges, it is likely that there will also be eight border sections. Make each of the sections and sew them into a complete circle. Sew the outer border to the inner circular star, matching the border points that meet the points of the circular star.

Drawing Flying Geese

The goose is loose! Think free! Think loose! Let your inhibitions go! This is one of the easiest designs to plan and to sew.

Basic Drawing

Start by outlining a general shape for your project, such as a square, a rectangle, or a free-form shape. Then fill the space with lines and circles. I often begin by drawing two concentric circles, which may form the basis for a star or a floating border. You can make the circles any size you want.

Use your flexible curve and draw some sweeping curves. After drawing the first curved line, keep your flexible curve in the same shape and use it to mirror the first line you've drawn. You will always need two more or less parallel lines to fill with geese (Figure 2–51).

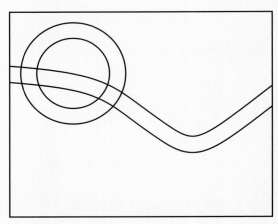

Figure 2–51.

Dividing the Sections

After you've added all the curved and straight lines you want, it's time to use your ruler to divide your sections for the geese. Keep in mind that the traditional Flying Geese block is half as tall as it is wide. Don't worry about making them exactly equal. Part of this project is the free spirit of each of your geese. After all, nothing in nature is exactly the same.

Angle the ruler as you go around curves. As sections become narrower, the geese become closer. Conversely, as the sections widen, the geese become farther apart (Figure 2–52).

Finding the Point

Now it is time to draw the triangle lines that form the individual geese. You can either place the triangle point mostly in the center or offset it.

Use your eye and a pencil to make a mark at the approximate center of each division. It is not necessary to find the exact center of each line. If your eye flows smoothly over the marks, then your marks are close enough to center (Figure 2–53).

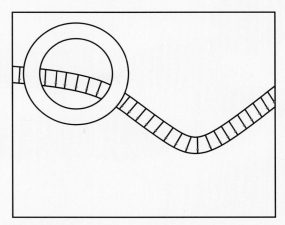

Figure 2–54.

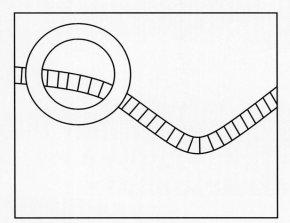

Figure 2–52.

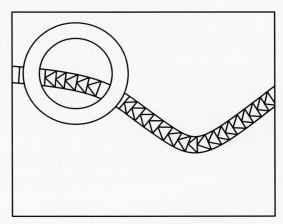

Figure 2–55.

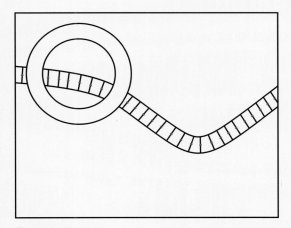

Figure 2–53.

For an offset point, choose an arbitrary measurement and make all the goose points there. For instance, if your section is 3" wide, you may opt to offset each point by 1". So, draw a point 1" from one side of each goose line (Figure 2–54).

Adding the Geese

Use a ruler or straight edge to draw in all of the geese lines (Figure 2–55).

For geese that are partially covered by another object in the drawing, draw dotted lines to rep-

resent the covered geese (Figure 2–56). Connect the lines, erasing everything that will be covered in the drawing (Figure 2–57 on the following page).

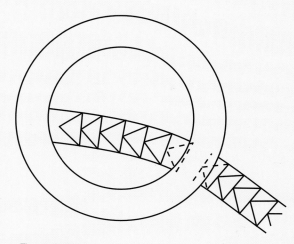

Figure 2–56.

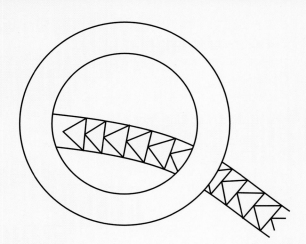

Figure 2–57.

In the finished drawing, it will appear that the geese flow smoothly from one edge of the drawing, beneath other objects, and off the other side (Figure 2–58).

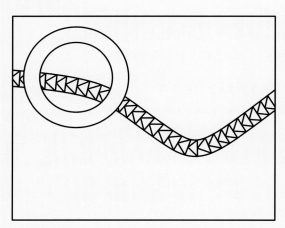

Figure 2–58.

Be cautious when drawing all of your curved and straight sections. Remember that you will need to sew what you draw. Watch for curves that are too sharp to sew easily and hopelessly interwoven strips. While these can be sewn, it may involve a lot of partially pieced seams, which translates into slow going at the machine.

Labeling the Pieces

Number each section in your drawing. Each individual part should have its own

number (Figure 2–59). For instance, the row of geese running through the illustrated drawing will be assembled in three different sections (sections 3, 5, and 6).

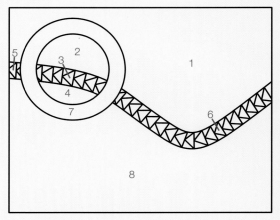

Figure 2–59.

Draw match marks to help align the points between oddly shaped sections. Place match marks closer together near curves and farther apart on straight or nearly straight edges. Be sure to mark every point where one design meets another. For instance, mark the circle at every point where a design element meets the edge of the circle, such as the intersections with the Flying Geese (Figure 2–60).

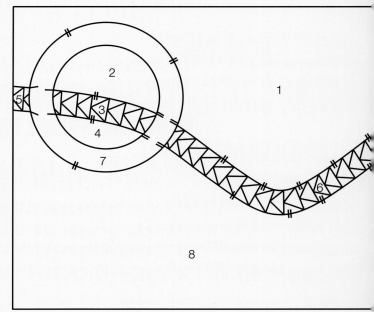

Figure 2–60.

Mirror Image or Identical?

Now is the time to decide if you want your completed quilt to exactly match the drawn design or to be a mirror image. Because Flying Geese are assembled by using paper-foundation piecing techniques, a mirror image will result. However, you can create an identical image if you first trace your design on the back of the drawing then trace the paper foundations from that side.

Foundation Piecing

Making foundations. Trace each design section on the dull side of the freezer paper, transferring all match marks (Figure 2–61). You can add seam allowances to the foundation, if you like. However, some quilters prefer to add the seam allowances to the fabric pieces by trimming the sewn sections to include the ¼" seam allowances after all of the geese have been sewn. It is necessary to make a paper foundation for every section of the design, even those that are one solid piece of fabric with no piecing.

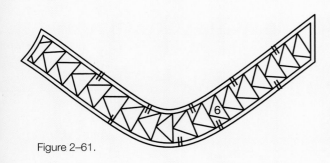

Figure 2–61.

Cutting fabric. Cut fabric strips at least ¾" wider than the tallest goose. For instance, if the tallest goose measures 1" from the base to the point, strips should be cut 1¾" wide (Figure 2–62).

Figure 2–62.

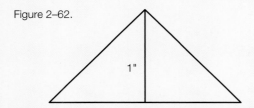

1"

Measure the short sides of the background triangles. Cut fabric strips at least 1¼" wider than the measurement for the largest triangle (Figure 2–63). Cut the strips into squares. The squares can then be cut in half on the diagonal.

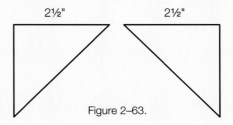

2½"   2½"

Figure 2–63.

Piecing Flying Geese. Use paper-foundation piecing techniques to assemble goose strips. The paper will be on the top, with the fabric below. Stitch the goose strip beginning with the bottom goose in the row. Always stitch geese in order from bottom to top (Figure 2–64). Use a short stitch to perforate the paper, making it easier to remove.

After sewing each seam, trim, and flip the pieces back and press them in place. The waxy coating on the freezer paper will melt and adhere to the fabric. Continue stitching until the entire strip is complete (Figures 2–65 through 2–72 on pages 40 and 41).

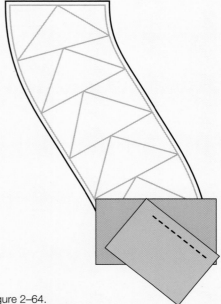

Figure 2–64.

Piecing Flying Geese, cont.

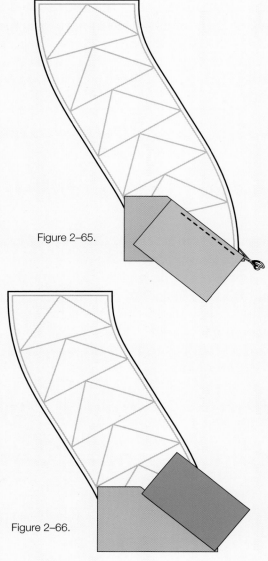

Figure 2–65.

Figure 2–66.

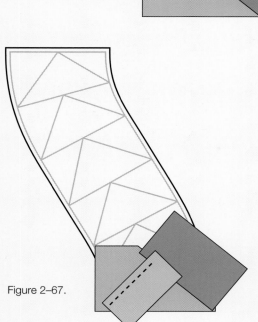

Figure 2–67.

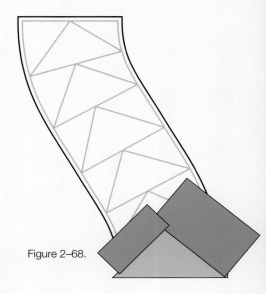

Figure 2–68.

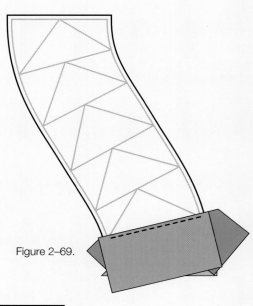

Figure 2–69.

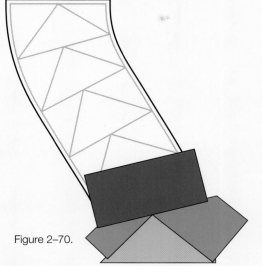

Figure 2–70.

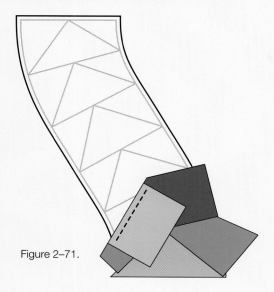

Figure 2–71.

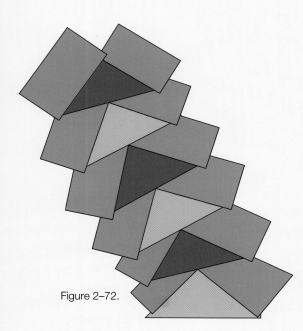

Figure 2–72.

Trimming sections. After each strip is complete, trim all edges to ¼" (Figure 2–73). I use a small ruler and rotary cutter to trim edges, but if you are uncomfortable using this equipment for this purpose, mark the ¼" seam allowance and trim the edges with scissors.

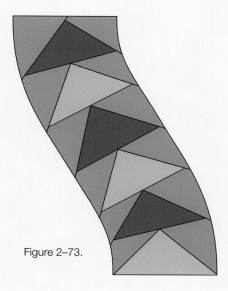

Figure 2–73.

Transfer match marks. Remove the paper from each section. Using a pencil, transfer all match marks to the wrong side of the fabric (Figure 2–74).

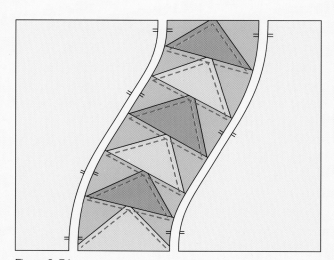

Figure 2–74.

Drawing Your Own Design

It's much easier than it would appear to draw your own circular star and Flying Geese quilt design. Draw one to three stars as described on pages 20 and 21. Cut a piece of paper (or tape pieces together) the size of the quilt you want to make. This will become your master pattern. Trace the outlines of the circles on the pattern wherever you want them. Add some parallel curved lines and draw Flying Geese in them as described on pages 36–38. Divide the rest of the background with simple curves or straight lines to indicate the placement of different fabrics.

Assembling the Sections

It is important never to cut up your master pattern. This is essential if one or more sections need to be replaced. From the master, make a paper foundation (described on page 26) for each section of your design, regardless of size. Even if the section contains no piecing and will be cut from one piece of fabric, it is important to have a paper pattern. I make all of my foundations from freezer paper.

Make match marks between each section on the master drawing. Also make a match mark where one section ends or adjoins another section. For instance, in Figure 2–75, mark the points on circle 25 where sections 26 and 27 meet the circle and where sections 29, 30, 31, and 32 meet circle 33. Make match marks in the areas where the circle meets the background. This is very helpful when inserting circles into the background. You can never add too many match marks. Transfer the match marks to each freezer paper section.

Foundation piece all the circular stars and the Flying Geese sections. Then, all that remains is sewing the sections together. I've used the basic design of COSMIC PARADE (page 65) to illustrate assembling the parts of a project.

Lay the sections face down in the order in which they will be assembled. Do not remove the

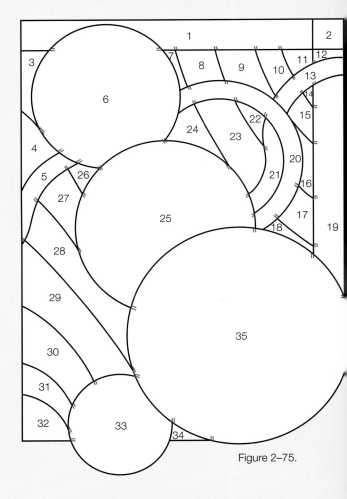

Figure 2–75.

paper until just before you are ready to join two sections. Transfer all match marks to the wrong side of the fabric pieces, remove the paper, and pin carefully, especially when piecing curves. Sew the seams with a ¼" seam allowance.

Piece small sections together to create larger units, then join the units to create the entire background. In most instances, the background needs to be completed before the circular stars with their borders are sewn into the whole (Figure 2–76 on the facing page).

Tip: When a partial star is part of the ove design, sew the entire star and then trim the correct size just before inserting it i the background. Double check the meas ment and the template you will use to the star to the correct size.

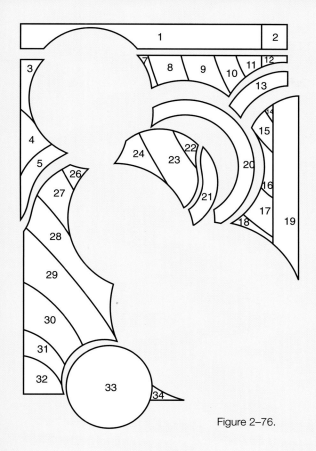

Figure 2–76.

I was astounded by the incredible machine-quilted masterpieces at the quilt shows I attended. It didn't seem possible that I could ever hope to excel at this technique. Then a funny thing happened. I began to relax at the sewing machine. I threw away all of my invisible nylon thread and replaced it with beautiful rayons and metallics. I gathered up my courage to try free-motion quilting without first marking the quilt top. Today, I use a variety of threads in each quilt and a combination of marked and free-form patterns. I no longer take short little stitches to start and stop a pattern. Instead, I leave a long thread tail, which I knot and pull between the layers.

Most of the quilts shown in this book were machine quilted. While I still love the look of hand quilting, there is simply not enough time in today's world to quilt everything by hand. There are many fine books with detailed instructions for both machine and hand quilting. The first decision must be whether to hand or machine quilt your project. This influences the type of batting to purchase.

Finishing Your Quilt

The top is done! It's time to celebrate! But wait, the fun isn't over yet. There is an old saying, "It's not finished until it's quilted." This is the point when many fine quilt tops move to the closet for all eternity.

It used to be that all of my quilts were hand-quilted. I was a traditionalist snob. I really enjoy hand work, and I love the effect of hand quilting. However, that was before the days of full-time work, travel, and home. Machine work became a necessity. My earliest attempts were rather pathetic. I mastered straight line, walking-foot stitching with ease but struggled with free-motion stitching. Over time, I learned a lot of tricks to camouflage my novice quilting: busy prints front and back, invisible nylon thread, and the ever popular stippling to fill in the background. My efforts remained mediocre.

Layer the Quilt

Tape or clamp the backing fabric, wrong side up, to a large surface. A tile floor or two work tables pushed together work well. Pull the backing fabric so it is taut. It should be free of bubbles and wrinkles. It should also be straight.

Tips:

1. I have a tile floor in my kitchen. I use the lines created by the tile edges as a guide, to make certain the backing is square.

2. I use #2 safety pins for basting. They are much easier to handle than smaller sizes, and I have never yet observed a permanent hole in a quilt from using this larger pin. These pins also adequately hold the layers in place. I have also never noticed a problem with slippage.

Lay the batting on top of the backing. Pat it in place, working from the center out toward the edges. Sometimes, creases in the batting can be removed by placing the batting in your dryer on the air-fluff setting. Always read the directions on the batting package before use. Do not pin the batting in place or attach it in any way to the backing.

Lay the quilt top, right side up, on top of the batting and backing. Baste the layers with the safety pins for machine-quilted projects and thread baste for hand-quilted projects. Work from the center out. First, baste vertically down the center of the quilt. Repeat at the horizontal center of the quilt. Then baste the diagonal lines. Last, baste a grid, both horizontally and vertically.

Thread

Use cotton, two-ply machine embroidery thread in the bobbin to help prevent the top threads from pulling through to the back. I use rayon or metallic threads for the quilt top. Rayon threads are used for the basic quilting, and metallic threads are used in selected areas for effect. Use variegated rayon if you will be crossing several colors of fabric. Otherwise, select a thread that closely matches the fabric color. Metallics are wonderful for effect, but they are notorious for causing stitching problems from broken threads to poor tension. However, the effect they provide outweighs their limitations.

Controlling Metallics

I use two different methods to offset some of the problems associated with metallic threads. First, I use a spindle to position the spool of metallic thread next to the machine, so that the thread rolls off the spool without twisting. The thread then passes over a small sponge, which can be soaked with a silicone lubricant. Place only a few drops of the silicone lubricant on the sponge. A little of this liquid goes a long way, so be careful not to overdo it. The thread is then

threaded normally in your sewing machine. My favorite needle for machine quilting with metallic threads is a denim needle. This needle is very sharp and has a large eye, which also helps to prevent thread breakage. If you do not have a denim needle, try an embroidery needle.

Starting and Stopping

Pull the bobbin thread to the top to begin stitching, both for walking-foot stitching and free-motion. Use a normal stitch length. At the end of the quilting line, leave a long tail on the top and back of the quilt. If your stitching begins or ends within the outermost seam allowance, which will be covered by the binding, then take several short stitches to lock the stitching in place.

After the quilting has been completed, pull all threads through from the back to the front of the quilt. Put a knot in each thread (I usually knot two together) about ½" away from the end of the stitching. Thread these through a large-eyed needle and slip them between the layers. Clip the tail ends of the thread.

Quilt as Desired

Now, there's a statement! It will be much easier if you approach the quilting one step at a time. Begin by stitching in the ditch between sections. This is the anchor stitching that holds everything in place and prepares the quilt for decorative stitching. After the sections are anchored, approach each section as if it were a small unique quilt. This helps me to remain focused on one area without feeling overwhelmed about the entire quilt.

Quilt the stars first. Generally, the individual pieces of a star are small. Often, they require nothing more than in-the-ditch stitching. Recently, I have begun adding little free-form swirls and loops to some of the points of my stars. I do not mark the quilt top, but sew approximately the same shape in each section. I was able to rationalize any imperfections by realizing that nothing in nature is perfectly symmetrical. The overall effect will be uniform. For some of the larger areas, I make a paper template to help keep my stitching focused. This template does not contain every stitched line, but rather acts as a guide. Cut out the template and spray the back of the paper with a spray adhesive that will allow the pieces to be repositioned. Quilt around the paper, being careful not to stitch through it. After the quilting has been completed, remove the paper template and move it to the next location. Each template can be used several times before the glue wears out.

Bind Your Quilt

Measure the length of both sides plus the width of the top and bottom of the quilt. Cut enough binding strips to go completely around your quilt. I prefer to make a double binding because it is more durable and easier to work with than a single layer of fabric. Cut 2½" wide binding strips either on the bias or crosswise grain of the fabric. Sew the strips together, end to end, with right sides together. If the strips were cut on the crosswise grain, sew them together at right angles and then trim the excess fabric. Press seam allowances open.

Press the binding strips in half, with wrong sides together. Attach the binding to the quilt top with raw edges aligned. Sew through all layers with a ¼" seam allowance. Turn the finished edge of the binding to the back, enclosing the raw edges of the quilt. Stitch in place by hand.

Make a Sleeve

If your quilt is intended to hang on the wall, you will want to make a sleeve for hanging. A sleeve is a strip of fabric that is generally 8½" wide and the length of the top of the quilt. Hem the ends of the strip and sew it into a long tube, right side out. Whipstitch the sleeve in place along the upper side of the back of the quilt. A dowel or curtain rod can be inserted through the sleeve to hang your finished quilt.

Sign Your Quilt

We have no way of knowing which of our quilts may last a hundred years. Quilt historians today lament the fact that the makers of many exquisite quilts will remain forever unknown merely because the quiltmaker did not have the foresight to place her name or some other identification on her masterpiece. We've also all heard the stories of "Aunt Mildred's" quilt collection, which was passed down to her by some maternal aunt or other unknown relative. Don't let this be the fate of your quilt. Be proud of it and take the time to place your name somewhere on the quilt, either the front or back. Do you have a star that didn't turn out quite as well as you would have liked? Sign it and stitch it to the back!

Close-up of COSMIC PARADE.

Close-up of COSMIC PARADE.

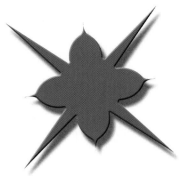

Chapter 3

Sample Projects

Here are some sample projects to get you started on making circular star and Flying Geese quilts. Enjoy the journey!

CELEBRATION STAR

CELEBRATION STAR

24" diameter

This Fourth of July CELEBRATION STAR is shown in shades of red, white, and blue. You will need four different shades of blue: dark, medium, light, and a background. From the red you will need dark, medium, and a background. For the best success, select fabrics with significant contrast between each shade.

Materials

Fabrics must be at least 40" wide. Additional yardage is necessary for any fabric less than 40".

Fabric	Yards
Blue	
Dark	½
Medium	¼
Light	⅛
Background 1	⅜
Red	
Dark	⅜
Medium	⅛
Background 2	⅛

Cutting Instructions

Color	Patches	Size
Blue		
Dark	8 F, 8 G	2" x 6"
Medium	8 D, 8 E	2½" x 7"
	8 N, 8 P	2" x 4"
	8 R	1½" x 2½"
Light	3 strips H	1½" x 30"
Background 1	8 B, 8 C	5" x 5"
	8 J, 8 K	2" x 4"
Red		
Dark	8 A	3½" x 5½"
	3 strips H	1½" x 30"
	8 S	2½" x 4½"
Medium	8 L, 8 M	2" x 4"
Background 2	8 Q	2" x 3½"

Sewing Instructions

The wedge is foundation pieced in two sections, and the piecing order is indicated by letters (full-size wedge pattern, pages 50–51). Make eight foundations for each section either by tracing the pattern on freezer paper or stacking four layers of freezer paper together and stitching on the sewing lines with no thread in your machine.

> **Tip:** Remember that the actual finished sta be a mirror image of the design shown i paper foundation piecing sections.

Section 1

1. Strip piece eight nine-patch blocks as shown in Figure 3–1. Be certain to use a scant ¼" seam allowance. The sewn block should measure 3½", including seam allowances.

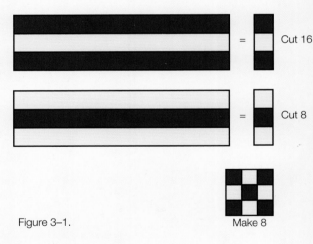

Figure 3–1.

Cut 16

Cut 8

Make 8

2. Baste the nine-patch block in the center of the Section 1 foundation.

3. Sew the remaining pieces in the order shown on the foundation.

Section 2

4. Sew the fabric pieces in the order shown on the foundation.

Putting It All Together

5. Remove the paper from each section. Sew Section 1 to Section 2, pinning intersections carefully to form one wedge of the star (Figure 3–2). Make eight wedges.

6. Sew four wedges together to form a half star. Repeat. Sew the two star halves together to complete the star.

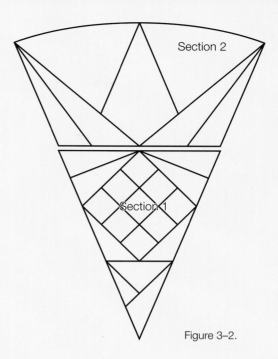

Figure 3–2.

Close-up of CELEBRATION STAR.

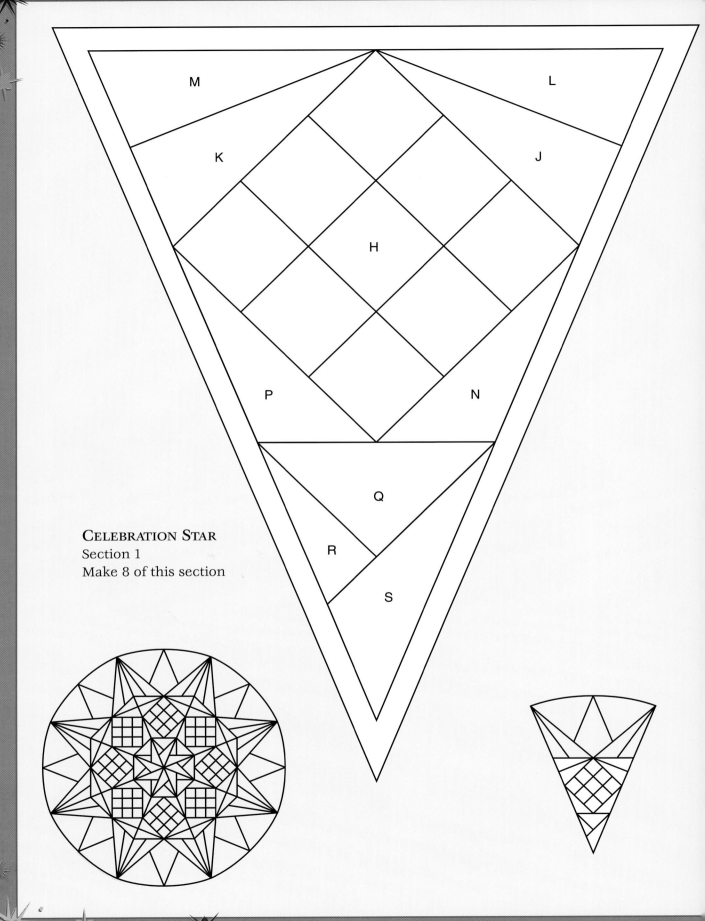

M

L

K

J

H

P

N

CELEBRATION STAR
Section 1
Make 8 of this section

Q

R

S

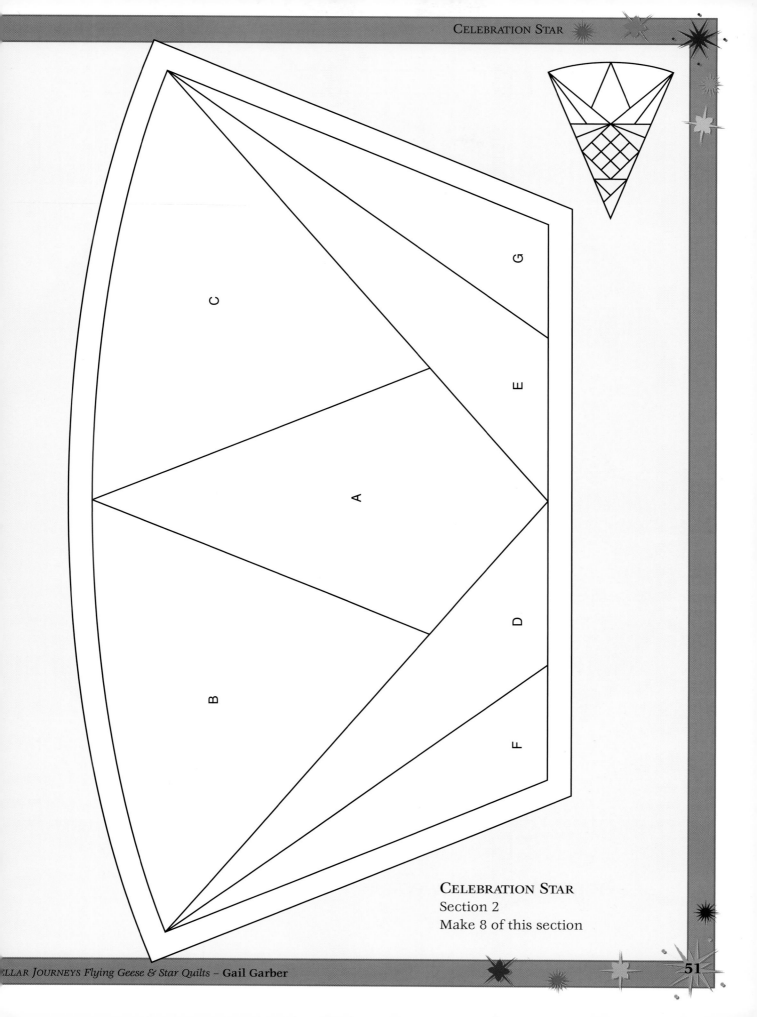

CELEBRATION STAR
Section 2
Make 8 of this section

NORTH BY NORTHWEST

NORTH BY NORTHWEST

24" diameter

This is the star in the upper-left corner of the quilt, COSMIC PARADE, on page 65. Here it is shown in shades of red and turquoise with a black background and a simple border.

Materials

Fabrics must be at least 40" wide. Additional yardage is necessary for any fabric less than 40".

Fabric	Yards
Turquoise	
Dark	¼
Light	¼
Stripe	⅛
Teal/red print	⅜
Red	1
Background	1½
Gold	¼

Cutting Instructions

Color	Patches	Size
Turquoise		
Dark	12 F	2½" x 4½"
Light	6 G, 6 K	3" x 7"
Stripe	6 L	use template*
Teal/red print	12 A	3¼" x 7"
Red	12 B, 12 C	2½" x 7"
	24 N	2" x 3"
	24 P	3" x 5"
Background		
	12 H, 12 J	4" x 6"
	24 M	2" x 4"
	24 Q	5" x 5"
Gold	12 D, 12 E	1½" x 7"

*Be sure to place the template for connecting piece L right side up on the right side of fabric.

Sewing Instructions

The sewing of this sample is shown in detail in the paper-foundation piecing section on page 26.

Sections

1. Using paper-foundation piecing, sew six each of Sections 1 and 2. These sections are alike except for pieces J and K, which have different shapes.

2. Trim the sections, leaving a ¼" seam allowance all around.

3. Remove the paper.

4. Sew Section 1 to Section 2, as shown in Figure 3–3, carefully matching points.

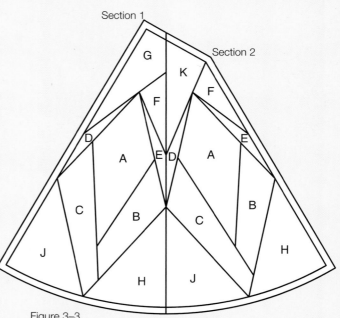

Figure 3–3.

5. Sew the connecting piece to the joined sections to complete the wedge (Figure 3–4).

Putting It All Together

6. Sew three wedges together to form a half circle. Repeat with the remaining wedges. Sew the two halves together to complete your circular star.

7. Stitch 24 border sections. Remove the paper. Piece these together to form a circle.

8. Sew the circular border to the circular star.

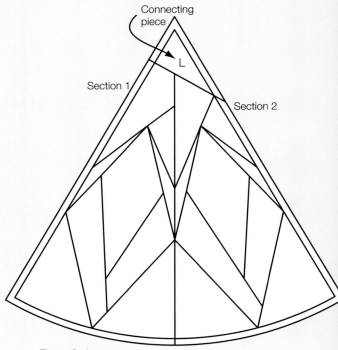

Figure 3–4.

Close-up of NORTH BY NORTHWEST.

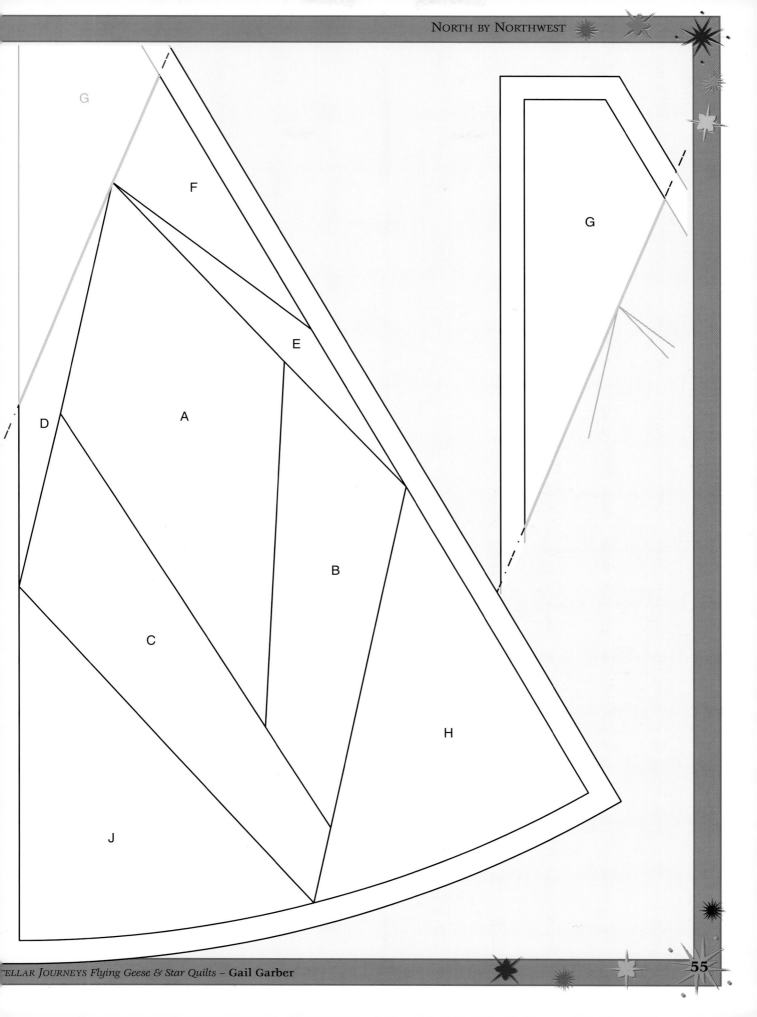

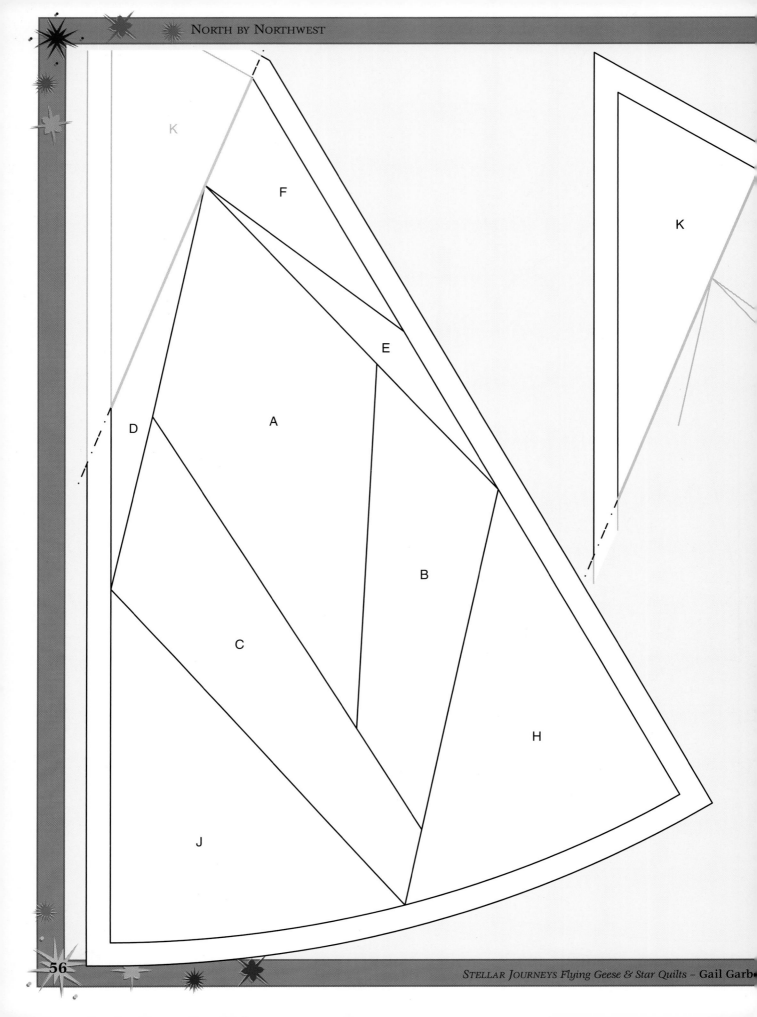

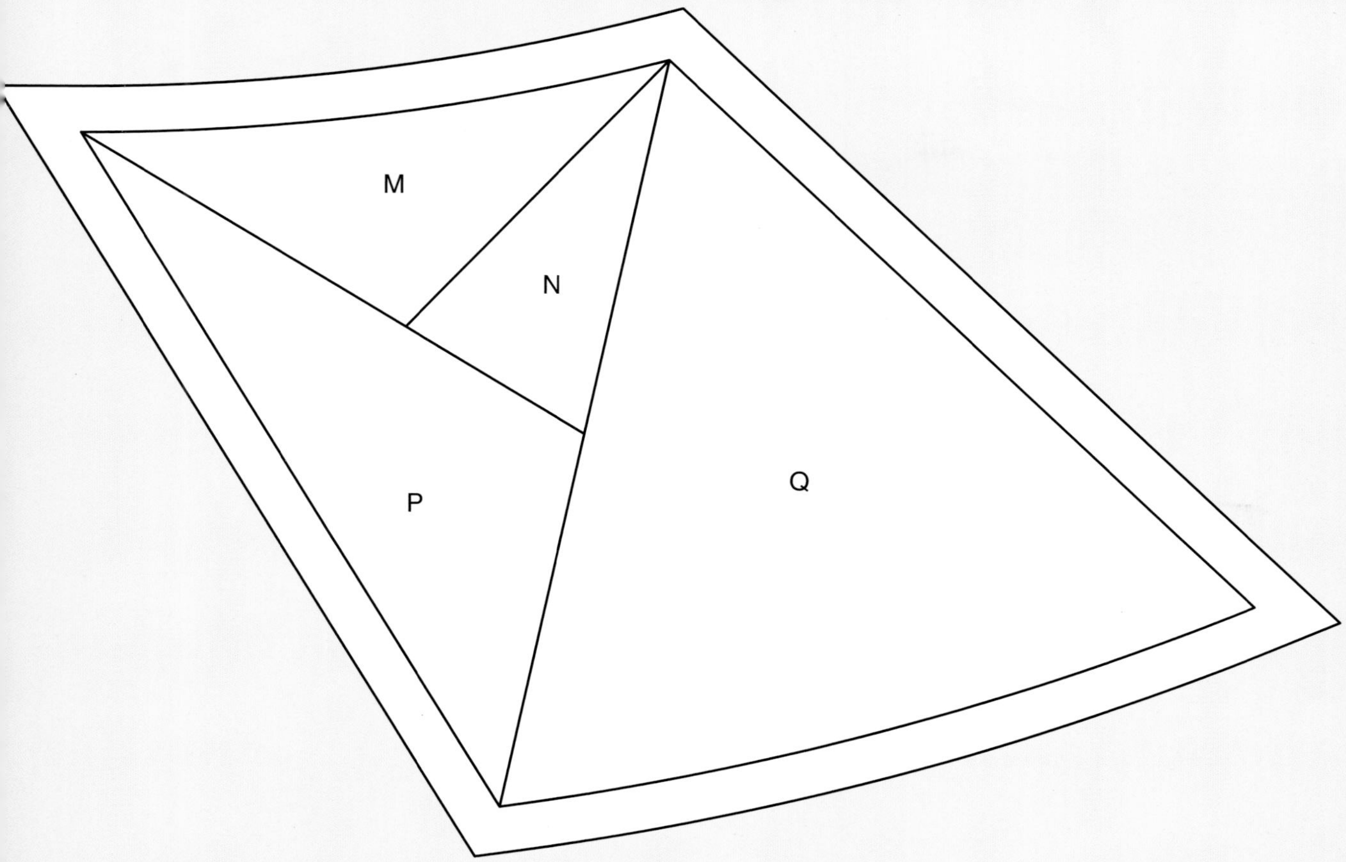

M

N

P

Q

L

G
K
F
E
A
B
C
H
J
M
N
P
Q

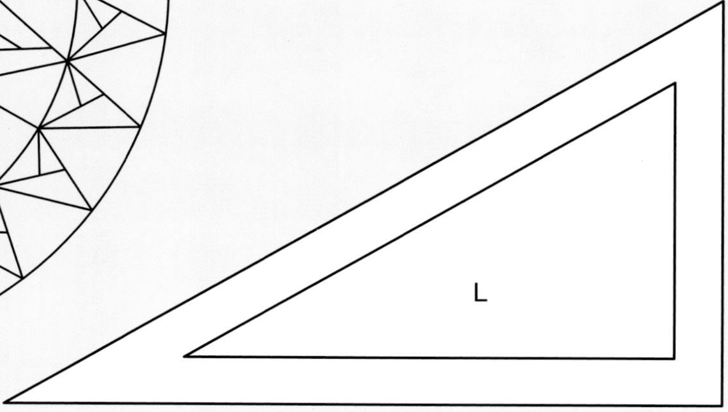

L

RIBBON GEESE

RIBBON GEESE

25" x 25"

My first thought was to use both the stars and the free-form geese, but then I decided to just let the loose goose stand alone. I designed a 7½" block and repeated it five times. The swirling geese become continuous when the blocks are connected.

Materials

Fabrics must be at least 40" wide. Additional yardage is necessary for any fabric less than 40".

Fabric	Yards
Light quilt background	1
Dark geese background	1
Includes border and binding.	
Assorted geese fabrics	scraps

Cutting Instructions

Color	Patches	Size
Backgrounds		
Light	20 CC	use template
	4 DD	5½" x 5½"
	4 EE	3" x 13"
Dark	80 squares	2½" x 2½"
	Cut squares	
	in half diagonally.	
Geese	Snip geese from	
	strips as you go.	

Sewing Instructions

1. Using paper-foundation piecing, sew 10 each of Sections 1 and 2 (see patterns on page 61).

2. Trim the sections, leaving a ¼" seam allowance all around.

3. Remove the paper.

Putting It All Together

4. Arrange the flying geese sections and CC patches in blocks (Figure 3–5).

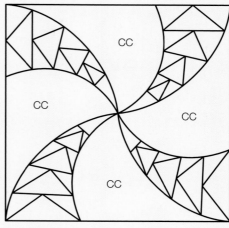

Figure 3–5.

5. Sew each Section 1 and 2 to a CC piece to make a CC unit. This is a relatively sharp curve. Mark the center point of each piece and pin heavily. Sew with the goose on top.

6. Sew two CC units together to form a half block. Then sew the two halves together.

7. Assemble the quilt top as shown in Figure 3–6. Sew the pieces together in numerical order, paying attention to the partial seams, as shown in the figure.

Partial Seams
Follow the piecing order as shown in Fig. 3–6. P1, P2, P3, and P4 with their arrows indicate where the partial seams need to remain unsewn until subsequent pieces have been added.

1. Join pieces 1 and 2, sewing from "start seam" to a couple of inches from the end of the seam (P1). Lock your stitches at P1 and at the end of every partial seam.

2. Sew piece 3 to pieces 1 and 2, then add piece 4.

Partial Seams cont.

3. Sew 5 and 6 together, leaving a partial seam at P2, as before.

4. Sew 5/6 to 2/4 and add piece 7.

5. Sew piece 8 to piece 1, stopping at P3.

6. Finish partial seam P1.

7. Join 9 and 10, stopping at P4.

8. Sew 9/10 to 5/8.

9. Sew 11 to 6/7 and finish P2.

10. Add 12 to 8/10 and finish P3.

11. Sew 13 to 9/11 and finish P4.

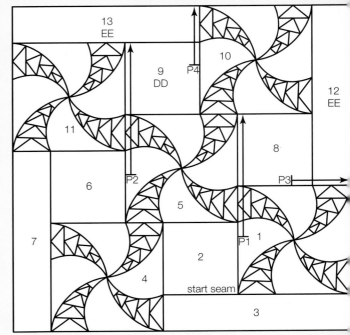

Figure 3–6.

Ribbon Geese block.

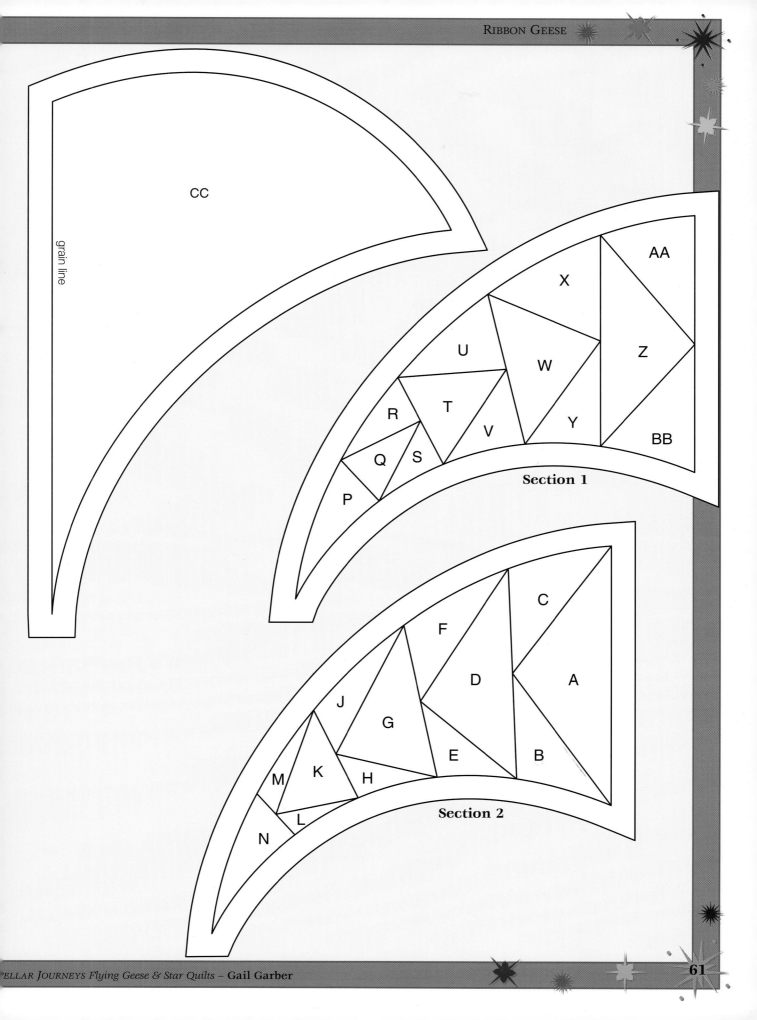

CC

grain line

AA

X

U

W

Z

R

T

V

Y

BB

Q

S

P

Section 1

C

F

D

A

J

G

E

B

M

K

H

N

L

Section 2

A Gallery of Stars

SPRING
48" x 48"
Made by the author

This quilt is one in a series of four made to show how a variety of star centers and borders can be mixed and matched to create several different quilts. The centers and borders in each quilt have the same dimensions. The circular borders feature a simple wash of fabric gradations and "flying diamonds."

STELLAR BOREALIS
24" diameter
Machine pieced, hand appliquéd, and
machine and hand quilted by the author

STELLAR BOREALIS was made as a chal[lenge]
quilt for my quilt guild. The inner sta[r has]
nine points rather than eight, and it be[came]
a piecing nightmare because of the [center]
point. In the end, I hand appliquéd one [disc]
over the seam for a more uniform look[. Flow-]
ing diamonds form the outer border.

AUTUMN
37" diameter
Machine pieced and quilted by the author

The second in the series, this small
quilt features the most simple, one-
patch border, "Swirls," along with a
double border of Flying Geese.

COSMIC PARADE
50" x 67"
Machine pieced and quilted by the author. Hand-dyed fabrics by Mickey Lawler.

It's a parade of colorful stars! The largest star in the lower-right corner represents the light of a rising star. The fractured background fades to dark in three stages as each star in the parade becomes more distant from the light source. Colorful geese wander throughout the parade. Perhaps they are the clowns that entertain the masses between star events. The author says that Mickey's fabrics helped her achieve the colorful effect and motion in the rows of Flying Geese.

BIG BANG

70" x 78"
Machine pieced and quilted by the author

This quilt is the first in my series of scrappy stars with a futuristic theme. The concept is two stars colliding. Both stars were to have been identical in the original plan, but once the first star was completed, it seemed boring and redundant to have two of the same. Besides, because the name suggests the beginning of our universe, two different stars seemed to be necessary, one in cool tones and the other in warm colors – opposing forces that meet in space. The free-form geese that fill in the background were an afterthought.

REDONDO – FULL-MOON RISING
60" x 75"
Machine pieced by author, machine quilted by Leta Brazell. This quilt is in the collection of Fairfield Processing Corporation.

Stars in motion pass in space amidst the chaos of the universe. Free-form geese trail from the largest star, forming a colorful tail, which is repeated in the partial border. This quilt was commissioned by Fairfield Processing and had to be completed in a short time. On a bitterly cold January day, I retreated to my cabin in the Jemez Mountains where I could sew in an inspirational setting. The name of the quilt reflects my surprise and delight to see the full moon rise over Redondo Peak during the first night.

JUNGLE LORD
59" x 39"
Machine pieced, hand
appliquéd, and machine
quilted by Patricia Drennan
Albuquerque, New Mexico

JUNGLE LORD is the third and last in a series of quilts made using free-form foundation-pieced Flying G
The randomly pieced geese make up the stripes in the tiger's body. The quilt is hand appliquéd and mac
quilted, and it has a small amount of couched embellishment. The design was inspired by a black and v
drawing of an Oriental tiger. If you look carefully, you will see the curve associated with the traditional
yang design. The tiger appears to be leaping from the dark into the light.

THE GOOSE IS LOOS
39" x 27"
This student work was
machine pieced and quilted
by Michele Hymel
Albuquerque, New Mexico

Michele was a student in Gail's The Goose-Is-Loose class. After the class, she was determined to finish
quilt, which took about two months to complete. She is now working on another loose-goose type of qu
an underwater scene.

PLANET OF THE GEESE
28" x 37"
Machine pieced and quilted by Anita McSorley
Albuquerque, New Mexico

This quilt began as an exercise in drawing free-form Flying Geese crossing over various sized circles drawn at random. Anita drew and colored four different variations before selecting the design. She hand-dyed all the fabrics used in this quilt. The black border is slightly discharged with bleach. The geese escaping into the border helped to incorporate the border into the body of the quilt, and the nine-patches at the intersections of the flights of geese add impact and an additional design element.

IF FROGS COULD FLY 2000
62" x 84"
Machine pieced and quilted by Cathy Combs
Albuquerque, New Mexico

IF FROGS COULD FLY is Cathy's first quilt. She purchased the batik frogs to make something for her daughter Shanna, who was beginning her second year at Texas Christian University (mascot is the Horned Frogs). She had already made a number of items in frog fabric for her. Her daughter was thrilled. Shanna is studying ballet and is a pre-med major. Because she has always stretched herself in everything she has tried, the quilt was named IF FROGS COULD FLY.

WILD FIRE
46" x 46"
Machine pieced and quilted by Alice Bessler, North Powder, Oregon. This quilt is in the author's collection.

The center star comes from the author's Four Star Quilts pattern, but the border is Alice's own design. The piece is heavily machine quilted with metallic and rayon threads, including stippled circular borders with stitches less than ⅛" apart. Alice is a popular teacher of machine quilting in Oregon.

CELESTIAL DRAGONS
58" x 50"
Hand appliquéd and hand
quilted by Pat Drennan
Albuquerque, New Mexico

CELESTIAL DRAGONS is the happy result of an immediate reaction to a small dragon in a collection of Oriental clip-art drawings. It was initially an experiment with the circular dragon worked as a single block. The trick was in utilizing the pieced triangles as an appliqué element for the dragon body. Dragon followed dragon, and work on this piece became a priority with FLOWER (p. 77) temporarily set aside.

SPRING BREEZE
50" x 64"
Machine-pieced, appliquéd,
and quilted by Page Gettman
Rio Rancho, New Mexico

Page chose a simple design for the star kite and let the fabrics create the appearance of motion. To enhance the illusion of twisting kite streamers, she used fabrics of different intensities to create a right-side-wrong-side effect. Smaller kites dance around the border where the sky progresses from bright daylight to the darkest night.

POSTCARD FROM OTAGO

52" x 63"

Machine pieced and quilted by Lidy Rekker, Dunedin, New Zealand. This quilt is in the author's collection.

POSTCARD FROM OTAGO is a wall-sized version of a larger quilt Lidy designed and stitched for her sports-mad nephew who lives in Australia. In his quilt, Lidy wanted to express the distance between them: ocean waves, wind, compass points. She also included New Zealand symbols like the fern leaf.

Lidy is a self-taught quiltmaker, who began quilting in 1984. Originally from the Netherlands, she came to New Zealand as a young adult. She began quilting after checking quilt books out from the library. When she began selling some of her quilts, she treated herself to a new book with each quilt sale, building a considerable library.

FLY ME TO THE STARS
Quilted garment
made by Kathy Morris
Albuquerque, New Mexico
modeled by Lisa Clark

…is project is Kathy's first design effort. It began as a wallhanging for her nephew, who wants to be an astro-…ut. Kathy converted the design to fit the garment. The title, FLY ME TO THE STARS, remains a tribute to her …phew. The long vest is from Judy Bishop's Pavilion Coat pattern.

…thy almost cannot remember a time when she didn't sew. As a child, her dolls wore dresses that were just …ces of cloth with holes cut for the arms with safety pins to hold everything together in the back. She made …r first dress at age 10. She made many of her clothes during high school, college, and career days. Several …ars ago, Kathy became intrigued with wearable art, mostly in the form of quilt pattern adaptations.

FLIGHT OF THE NIGHT GEESE
Quilted garment
Made by Harriet Smith
Albuquerque, New Mexico
modeled by Lisa Clark

…e inspiration for this jacket came from Gail Garber's Milagro Jacket pattern, which seemed like the perfect …ce to put Flying Geese and stars. Following in her mother's footsteps, Harriet began making garments on …readle sewing machine more than 50 years ago. After her children settled in their own homes, her interest …ned to quilting and embellishing wearables. Now that her husband has retired, Harriet spends much of …r time at their cabin in northern New Mexico, where she can sew in the peace and quiet of the Sangre …Cristo Mountains.

MESA VERDE: CALLING HOME THE ANASAZI

59" x 70"

Machine pieced, hand stamped, and machine quilted by Anita Marsh McSorley, Albuquerque, New Mexico. Hand-dyed fabrics by De Lunn, stamps by the author and Katie Widger.

It was love at first sight and touch for Anita when, at age 10, she was allowed to assist her moth and great-aunt at a county fair quilt show. Her mother taught her to sew shortly after, and she has stopped since. It was during the 1970s that she sewed her first quilt as a gift for her nephew. Whe she moved to Albuquerque in 1989, she finally had time to devote to her love affair with quilts.

Anita's second love is New Mexico and its history. She was inspired to design this quilt after readi about the disappearance of the Anasazi Indians from their cliff dwellings. Archaeologists still se the answer to this mystery.

MIGRATION
39" x 58"
Machine pieced and quilted
by Dolores J. Millard
Albuquerque, New Mexico

Inspiration for this quilt came during an autumn visit to Bosque del Apache National Wildlife Refuge in south-central New Mexico. This refuge is home to tens of thousands of wintering waterfowl. The cranes and geese were flying overhead in a perfectly formed "V" formation that seemed to go on forever.

Dolores began sewing in 4-H and home economics at the age of 10. Her real interest in quilting began about four years ago, and since then she has created 10 to 12 quilts a year in addition to working more than full-time.

GEESE IN MOTION
49" x 38"
Made by Helen Goesling Duncan
Albuquerque, New Mexico

Helen is proud of the quilting genes in her family. Unfortunately, she never had the opportunity to meet either of her great-grandmothers who excelled at it. Helen began quilting about 30 years ago when she made her first quilt as a required project in a college art class. Helen created the design for this quilt as she progressed, and her main goal throughout the project was to keep the quilt small.

ROCKY MOUNTAIN RAPTORS
66" x 68"
Designed and machine quilted by the author

This quilt top was stitched in one day by eight dedicated staff and volunteers, four men and four women, of Hawks Aloft, Inc. They used paper-foundation piecing, machine appliqué, and traditional piecing techniques. It is the seventh annual fund-raising quilt for this nonprofit organization. Featuring photo transfers in a contemporary attic windows setting, the quilt is complemented by an appliquéd landscape in some of the blocks. It also contains a single row of free-form Flying Geese encircling the center. Several different feather prints enhance the overall theme of the raptors. The photo transfers were done by Marvin and Jeannie Spears of Picture Perfect Fotos on Fabric.

FLOWER
29" x 34"
Hand appliquéd and machine quilted by Pat Drennan, Albuquerque, New Mexico

Pat is essentially a self-taught quilter, having started at a time when little was available to the novice. Appliqué has been the driving force in her work since 1991 and remains her chosen focus. FLOWER is an attempt at combining appliqué, foundation piecing, and decorative machine quilting. It was inspired by the author's demonstration of scrappy foundation piecing of the irregular Flying Geese and was a response to her challenge to come up with an original interpretation. This little quilt did not come to life until the wispy fringe was added to the flowers.

A Bug's View
39" x 32"
Machine pieced and quilted by Susie Gray, Tijeras, New Mexico

This quilt began in response to the author's challenge to find a unique way to use curved Flying Geese. Susie wanted to create a landscape quilt but was having difficulty incorporating geese into it. One evening while watching "A Bug's Life" with her daughter Abby, she suddenly saw the blades of grass as flying geese intertwined with giant dandelions. The addition of the bugs was her daughter's idea.

About the Author

Gail Garber began quilting in 1980 after her friends encouraged her to take a hand-quilting class. She had little idea that this small step would have a major impact on her life. Now she lectures and teaches workshops for quilt guilds and shops throughout the United States and abroad.

She began publishing Southwestern design patterns in 1988, followed by a series of star designs and garments. She has written numerous magazine articles in the U.S. as well as Japan, New Zealand, France, and the United Kingdom.

When she is not quilting, Gail is the executive director of Hawks Aloft, Inc., a New Mexico nonprofit organization that specializes in bird research and environmental education. Gail can often be found in the back country of New Mexico, studying birds like the ferruginous hawk and golden eagle, and conducting surveys of small songbirds such as the endangered Southwestern willow flycatcher.

Hawks Aloft naturalists, accompanied by non-releasable raptors, visit New Mexico classrooms every day of the school year, teaching young people about the importance of preserving habitat for wildlife. Several of the birds in the program reside in large flight cages behind Gail's home.

Gail feels fortunate to be able to pursue her favorite activities in life, creating quilt designs, working with birds, and exploring the little-known and seldom-seen parts of her home state.

Gail Garber
began quilting in 1980
after her friends *encouraged* her
to take a hand-quilting class.
She had little *idea*
that this small step
would have a *major impact*
on her *life*.

Other AQS Books

This is only a small selection of the books available from the American Quilter's Society. AQS books are known worldwide for timely topics, clear writing, beautiful color photos, and accurate illustrations and patterns. The following books are available from your local bookseller, quilt shop, or public library.

#5850   US$21.95

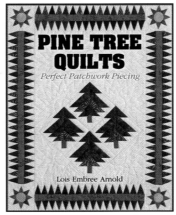

#5708   US$22.95

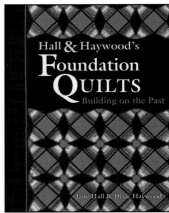

#5707   US$26.95

#5176   US$24.95

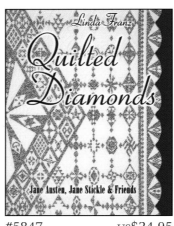

#5847   US$24.95

#5764   US$19.95

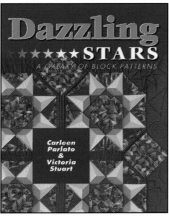

#5844   US$21.95

#5761   US$22.95

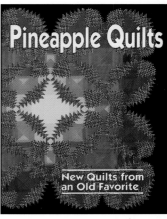

#5098   US$16.95

Look for these books nationally or call **1-800-626-5420**